TIMESAVER FOR EXAM

PHOTOCOPIABLE

Reading and Use of English

FOR FIRST (FCE)

By Fiona Davis

Contents

Introduction

Who is this book for?

This book is for teachers of students who are preparing for the Reading and Use of English test in the *Cambridge English: First* or *Cambridge English: First for Schools* exam and who require extra practice material. Ideal as a supplement to any First Certificate or upper-intermediate coursebook, the topics and activities are especially designed to appeal to older teenage and young adult classes. This resource is also suitable for use with any upper-intermediate classes who wish to broaden their vocabulary and develop their reading skills at B2 level.

The *Cambridge English: First* exam – an overview

Cambridge English: First is a qualification at upper-intermediate level (Level B2 on the CEFR scale) which is officially recognised by universities, employers and governments around the world. The exam is aimed at learners who want to use English for study at an upper-intermediate level, start working in an English-speaking environment, or live independently in an English-speaking country.

The exam consists of four tests: Reading and Use of English, Writing, Listening, and the Speaking Test.

Students will be given one hour and fifteen minutes to do the **Reading and Use of English** test, which is divided into seven parts. Parts 1 to 4 contain tasks with a grammar and vocabulary focus. Parts 5 to 7 contain a range of texts with accompanying reading comprehension tasks. Task types are as follows:

How does this book help your exam students?

- The *Cambridge English: First* exam requires students to have a wide-ranging vocabulary. The activities in this book provide useful practice to help broaden your students' lexical knowledge. For example, there are activities focussing on confusing words, common collocations, multi-word verbs, noun forms and commonly tested items.
- The lessons in this book help students to develop important *First* reading skills such as understanding the development of a text by recognising coherence ar cohesion devices, skimming and scanning techniques and understanding attitude and opinion.
- Practice of discrete exam task types is crucial for all students, whatever their level, and there are many activities of this kind in this book. For example, in Part 1 using a logical process of elimination can help students with multiple-choice questions, and in Part 3 students are provided with the opportunity to manipulate word families which is essential for the word formation task.
- There are activities to develop students' reading skills for the second part of the exam (Parts 5–7), for example, showing students the usefulness of predictio in approaching the multiple-choice task and encouragi students to look for synonyms and paraphrases to help them with the multiple-matching task.
- Handy exam tips remind students of strategies which will help them in their actual exam and also offer advic on study skills relevant to the exam.

PART	TASK TYPE	
1	Multiple-choice cloze	a short text with eight gaps: there are multiple-choice options for each of the gaps
2	Open cloze	a short text with eight gaps for students to complete
3	Word formation	a short text with eight gaps: students complete the sentences by changing each of the word stems provided
4	Key word transformation	six sentences: students use given key words to rewrite the sentences whilst retaining the meaning
5	Multiple-choice	a reading text followed by six multiple-choice comprehension questions
6	Gapped text	a text from which six sentences have been removed: students match the sentences to the gaps in the text
7	Multiple matching	ten statements/questions which are to be matched to paragraphs in a text or several short texts

- Understanding the reasoning behind exam questions is valuable for students, enabling them to look at the exam from another point of view. Some of the activities in this book give students the opportunity to 'Be the examiner!' – such as deciding what words should be gapped in an open cloze.

- As the total length of the texts in the *Cambridge English: First* exam is around 2,200 words, students need to be able to read quickly and accurately. Activities marked with this stopwatch symbol are designed to help students increase their reading speed.

- Many of the practice activities include a clearly signposted **EXAM TASK**. These exam-style activities incorporate language which has been the focus of the preceding activities in an authentic exam task format. The exam tasks would also be appropriate for doing as timed practice of a discrete exam task type.

An authentic practice exam at the end of the book is also provided with full answer key.

Iow do I use this book?

ach lesson provides practice for one particular part of the xam and the activities are grouped accordingly. Use the ssons to supplement your coursebook by providing extra ractice of a difficult area or some variety in how a language ea is approached. *Timesaver for Exam* activities can also e used to provide an introduction to an exam task, skill or xical area.

The activities are designed to be teacher-led, but are used without separate Teacher's notes. Clear instructions are on the pages, which are all photocopiable.

The part, question type and lesson focus are clearly labelled at the top of each lesson.

This symbol 60 mins gives an approximate lesson length, but please note that timings may vary according to class size, level of language, etc.

The comprehensive answer key at the back of the book provides an explanation of the answers.

Where appropriate, students are asked to work in pairs or small groups to generate more language and to engage students further in the tasks.

Some activities include cards which will need to be cut out as preparation for the class. Cutting lines and fold lines are clearly marked.

e hope you enjoy the variety in these activities and that ey will add to your students' enjoyment of learning glish for the *Cambridge English: First* exam.

The Timesaver series

The Timesaver series provides hundreds of ready-made lessons for all levels, topics and age groups. Other *Timesaver for Exams* titles are available for the Listening and Writing exams. Check out these and other Timesaver titles at **www.scholastic.co.uk/elt**.

Play fifty-fifty

Pair A

1 **You have the answers for sentences a–f. Pair B can get a maximum of four points for each sentence.**

a) laid / lay / let / lied

She *laid* the towel on the beach so that it could dry out.

b) beat / lose / score / win

We need to *beat* this team by two points to get to the final.

c) recalled / recognised / remembered / reminded

The police showed the witness photos of five women and he *recognised* the face of the robber in the photo immediately.

d) at the moment / at present / nowadays / presently

Please take a seat. The doctor will be here *presently*. She's just seeing another patient.

e) amount / number / rate / size

Environmentalists are very concerned about the *amount* of pollution which is being dumped at sea.

f) Although / Despite / However / Whereas

Despite not having a track to practise on, the running team from Hamilton finished first.

Exam tip!

For each multiple-choice item, first cross out the answers which are definitely wrong. Then choose the correct answer.

2 **Look at each sentence. Discuss and cross out two incorrect answers. Tell Pair B which pair of words you have left. If the pair contains the correct answer, you get two points. Decide on the final answer. Check with Pair B. This is worth two more points.**

a) All / Both / Every / Neither

.... my parents work in the hospital.

b) brought / fetched / obtained / taken

'Hi, Noah. Let's go into the theatre. Have you .... your ticket with you?'

c) contrary / contrast / opposite / other hand

Unemployment is not going down. On the ...., job losses in the manufacturing industry are on the increase.

d) collect / earn / gain / receive

They .... their living by taking tourists round the historical sites.

e) achieved / managed / succeeded / won

Japanese scientists have .... in transmitting electricity wirelessly.

f) watched / noticed / observed / remarked

I was looking for a Saturday job when I .... an advert for a waiter in a shop window.

Pair B

1 Look at each sentence. Discuss and cross out two incorrect answers. Tell Pair A which pair of words you have left. If the pair contains the correct answer, you get two points. Decide on the final answer. Check with Pair A. This is worth two more points.

a) laid / lay / let / lied

She .... the towel on the beach so that it could dry out.

b) beat / lose / score / win

We need to .... this team by two points to get to the final.

c) recalled / recognised / remembered / reminded

The police showed the witness photos of five women and he .... the face of the robber in the photo immediately.

d) at the moment / nowadays / at present / presently

Please take a seat. The doctor will be here .... She's just seeing another patient.

e) amount / number / rate / size

Environmentalists are very concerned about the .... of pollution which is being dumped at sea.

f) Although / Despite / However / Whereas

.... not having a track to practise on, the running team from Hamilton finished first.

2 You have the answers for sentences a–f. Pair A can get a maximum of four points for each sentence.

a) All / Both / Every / Neither

Both my parents work in the hospital.

b) brought / fetched / obtained / taken

'Hi, Noah. Let's go into the theatre. Have you *brought* your ticket with you?'

c) contrary / contrast / opposite / other hand

Unemployment is not going down. On the *contrary*, job losses in the manufacturing industry are on the increase.

d) collect / earn / gain / receive

They *earn* their living by taking tourists round the historical sites.

e) achieved / managed / succeeded / won

Japanese scientists have *succeeded* in transmitting electricity wirelessly.

f) watched / noticed / observed / remarked

I was looking for a Saturday job when I *noticed* an advert for a waiter in a shop window.

Exam tip!

For each multiple-choice item, first cross out the answers which are definitely wrong. Then choose the correct answer.

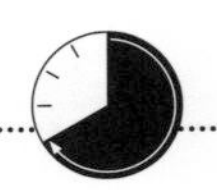

The common cold

1 **Work in pairs: A and B. Look at the phrases in your box only and look up any unfamiliar words.**

Pair A

the common cold the general public the human body
a high fever an infectious disease a routine check a sore throat

Pair B

the average adult blood cells close contact a leading cause
a runny nose severe symptoms standard practice

2 **Take it in turns to describe one of the phrases from your box.**
Don't **use either of the words from the collocation in your definition.**
Can your partner guess which of the phrases you are describing?

3 **Fold here or cover exercises 1 and 2 as you do the exam task.**

Exam tip!

Collocations are words that are often used together. When you learn a new adjective, find out which nouns it is used with.

Fold here *Fold here*

EXAM TASK

4 **For questions 1–8, read the text below and decide which answer (A, B, C or D) best fits each gap.**

A cold is known as the **(0)** ...common... cold for a reason. It is the most frequent **(1)** .... disease in humans. The **(2)** .... adult suffers from a cold two to four times a year. Children often get between five and seven colds a year due to their **(3)** .... contact with other children. Although colds are usually relatively mild, they are a **(4)** .... cause of doctor visits and absences from school and work. The symptoms of a cold are a **(5)** .... throat and a runny nose. A cold begins when a cold virus attaches to the lining of the nose or throat. Your immune system sends white blood **(6)** .... to attack this germ. As a result, the nose and throat become inflamed and produce mucus. See your doctor if you have a **(7)** .... fever or muscle aches. More **(8)** .... symptoms may mean you have flu instead.

0	**A** ordinary	**B** normal	**C** common (circled)	**D** general
1	**A** harmful	**B** infectious	**C** poisonous	**D** unhealthy
2	**A** average	**B** common	**C** general	**D** routine
3	**A** near	**B** close	**C** nearby	**D** local
4	**A** main	**B** vital	**C** first	**D** leading
5	**A** sore	**B** stiff	**C** severe	**D** sharp
6	**A** organisms	**B** units	**C** parts	**D** cells
7	**A** sharp	**B** serious	**C** high	**D** deep
8	**A** strong	**B** severe	**C** heavy	**D** powerful

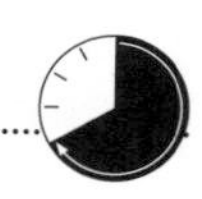

Telling barefaced lies

1 **Match the idioms in the text with the definitions. There are two alternatives that you don't need.**

My earliest memories are of my grandmother. Whenever I visited with my parents, she would be outside in the garden, **(1)** putting her back into some project or other: digging, landscaping, tending plants, bringing her dreams to life whatever the weather. When my parents died in a road accident, she welcomed me with open arms. But looking after me wasn't an easy task. I was always **(2)** up to my neck in trouble, whether it was stealing sweets or **(3)** telling barefaced lies. She **(4)** kept her head, no matter what I did, and in time I learned to follow her example. I never inherited her **(5)** green fingers, but I learned from her that whatever you do, you should do it **(6)** with all your heart. And never **(7)** turn your back on those you love.

a) with all your energy and emotion ......6......
b) be in a situation that it is hard to get out of ....
c) not help or support ....
d) not doing your best at ....
e) stayed calm ....
f) love of plants and making them grow ....
g) not telling the truth and not ashamed of it ....
h) being impatient ....
i) working very hard at ....

2 **Work in four small groups: A–D. Your teacher will give each group a list of three idioms. Find the definition of the first idiom and put it into an example sentence. Then invent two more definitions and example sentences. Make sure your definitions are likely! Do the same for the other two idioms on the list.**

3 **Read out your sentences and definitions to another group. Can they guess the correct meaning? If they guess correctly, they score a point. If they don't, the point is yours!**

Group A
keep your head down
catch someone red-handed at something
be up to your ears in something

Group C
keep an eye on someone / something
pull someone's leg
have the cheek to do something

Group B
stick your neck out
be up in arms about something
get cold feet

Group D
turn a blind eye to something
break someone's heart
have no stomach for something

On my way

1 **Complete the sentences with *direction(s), way, path(s)* or *track*.**

a) I'm looking for the town centre. Am I going in the right ......*direction*...... ?

b) We're a long .... from home.

c) I used to see Ginny a lot, but after I changed job, our.............................. didn't cross again.

d) The quickest .... to the station is down London Road.

e) The police are on the .... of the robber.

f) The new house was perfect. We walked excitedly up the .... to the front door.

g) Do you know the .... back?

h) A passerby asked me for .... to the station.

i) The government seems to be on the right .... as crime rates are going down at last.

j) Sally started out making tea for the actors and worked her .... up to producing some of the theatre's best plays.

2 **Write the phrases on the mind map.**

Am I going in the right direction?

DIRECTION(S)

WAY

TRACK

PATH

Exam tip!

Multiple-choice options are often similar. Learn similar groups of words in context, putting each in an example sentence. You can record the phrases on a mind map.

3 **Draw a mind map using one of the sets of nouns and examples: A or B.**

look glance sight view

A

Take a look at this photo! *The view* from the top of the building was stunning.

I *caught sight of* him waiting at the information desk. She gave him *a quick glance* and smiled.

At first glance, the restaurant didn't seem to be very busy. She *gave* the man *a* long, hard *look*.

In my view, we need to change the rules on airport tax. They're going to Tokyo to see *the sights*.

I didn't like *the look of* the cut on her hand.

When the runway *came into view*, everyone in the plane cheered.

journey travel(s) trip expedition

B

The writer met a lot of new people *on her travels* in the USA. Have *a safe journey*!

Expeditions to the North Pole are getting increasingly dangerous. *Travel* is my favourite pastime.

We're off on *a day trip* to the seaside. *Air travel* is safe and getting safer.

Check out the website for the latest *travel information*. We started *the long journey* home.

The *journey* to the lakes took all day. I'm on a *business trip* to Frankfurt next week.

4 **Compare your mind maps in pairs. Add more examples if you can.**

EXAM TASK

5 **For questions 1–8, read the text below and decide which answer (A, B, C or D) best fits each gap.**

The hidden cove

The village was not as I had imagined. A fellow student I had met on my **(0)** ...*travels*... advised me to go there. Although our **(1)** .... didn't cross again, I was determined to take up his recommendation. It was a long bus **(2)** .... to get there and when the first buildings came into **(3)** .... through the coach's dusty windows, I thought I had made a mistake.

The hotel was a modern block with very little character. The owner seemed disinterested and didn't give me more than a very brief **(4)** .... before handing over my key. For the first time in my month away, I felt a very long **(5)** .... from home.

I set off in what I thought was the right **(6)** .... for the beach and this time I was not disappointed. The **(7)** .... leading to the beach was between pine trees. When I first caught **(8)** .... of the bay on the other side, it took my breath away. It was the perfect hidden cove, and there was no other tourist to be seen.

0	**A** trips	**(B)** travels	**C** journeys	**D** expeditions
1	**A** travels	**B** directions	**C** roads	**D** paths
2	**A** voyage	**B** travel	**C** tour	**D** journey
3	**A** view	**B** look	**C** watch	**D** glimpse
4	**A** glance	**B** view	**C** sight	**D** regard
5	**A** path	**B** way	**C** route	**D** road
6	**A** way	**B** line	**C** track	**D** direction
7	**A** street	**B** direction	**C** path	**D** course
8	**A** view	**B** look	**C** sight	**D** glimpse

Your smartphone – best friend or worst enemy?

1 **Read what Dee says about smartphones. Do you agree with her?**

Dee Foster, 17

What I hate most about smartphones, is going out to a restaurant with someone **who** loves theirs! There's nothing **worse than** when your friend puts their phone on **the** table. They are always expecting a message, and it gets in the way of conversation. And it's **so** rude when **someone** interrupts you to look up something on their phone. I think we should all take a smartphone break **from** time to time. Next time you're going for a pizza, text your friend and tell them you're leaving your phone at home and suggest they **do** too!

2 **Look at the words in bold in these sentences and match them with the grammar points.**

1 I've got a new smartphone and my best friend's got **one** too.
2 Have you got his number **in** your phone?
3 The camera is **not as good as** yours.
4 Look at the colour. I love **it**!
5 This is **such** a great video!
6 Why don't you post **a** comment?
7 You should get a phone **which** has a better camera.

a) pronoun
b) article
c) relative pronoun
d) substitution
e) comparison
f) preposition
g) emphasis

3 **Now find more examples from Dee's text. Match the words in bold with the grammar points a–g.**

a) pronoun ……someone……
b) article ……………
c) relative pronoun ……………
d) substitution ……………
e) comparison ……………
f) preposition ……………
g) emphasis ……………

Exam tip!

Answers for the cloze in Part 2 of the exam are always one word only.

4 **BE THE EXAMINER! Work in pairs: Pair A or Pair B. Read a text (A or B) giving another opinion on smartphones. Take a black pen and make six gaps (one word in each gap). Cross out only the types of words from exercises 2 and 3.**

5 **Each Pair A works with a Pair B. Swap texts and complete the gaps.**

6 **Compare your answers. Sometimes more than one answer may be possible – check with your teacher. Which gaps were easiest to complete? Which were more difficult? Why?**

A

Tara Subramaniam, 17

I love my smartphone. I couldn't live without one! But everywhere you look, people are glued to their screens and missing opportunities to notice and appreciate the world around us. This smartphone addiction seriously affects our ability to focus too. I can't even watch a movie without checking my phone, which means nothing ever gets my full attention.

I also worry I depend on my phone too much. I use to-do lists to organise my studies and the maps apps for getting to places. It was a relief when I went on a school trip last year and couldn't use my phone. I survived for a week! Try it – you'll be surprised. Your brain can be just as powerful as Google!

B

Danny Fratelli, 16

Smartphones are the best! Smartphones encourage us to think more and are an infinite source of information. They are a great way to research topics we hear others talking about. Say you're with your friends and they're discussing a current event you know nothing about. You can use your phone to find the information you need and even take part in the conversation.

Smartphones are brilliant for finding people who have the same interests as me. For example, I really love making YouTube videos, but nobody at my school does. My phone allows me to connect with other YouTubers and learn from them too.

Having fun for free!

1 **Work in groups of three: Student A, Student B and Student C. Write the answer to each of your questions on a piece of paper. Each question practises an *adjective/verb + preposition*. Don't include the adjective or verb in the answer.**

Example question: What are you **addicted to**? Why?

Example answer: *Chili pepper. I love the taste and have it with every meal.*

2 **Read each of your answers to your classmates. They listen and guess which *adjective/verb + preposition* you are describing. They can use the prompt sheet to help them.**

Student A

1. Name one thing you are **skilled at**. Why do you think this is?
2. Name someone in the class who has been **kind to** you. What did they do?
3. What are you **interested in**? How do you find out about this?
4. What did you last **complain about**? Why?
5. What is your favourite smell? What does it **remind you of**?

Student B

1. Name something you are **bored with** doing. Say why this is.
2. In your family, who are you **similar to**? In what ways?
3. What were you **thinking about** before you came into the class?
4. Can you think of someone who you often **disagree with**? Why do you think this is?
5. What are you sometimes **frightened of**? Why?

Student C

1. Name something you are **proud of**. Why is this?
2. Name something you get **anxious about**. Why do you think this is?
3. Where did you last go out for a meal? Whose turn was it to **pay for** it?
4. What was the last thing you had to **wait for**? How long did you have to wait?
5. At work or at home name one thing you are **responsible for**. How do you feel about this?

PROMPT SHEET

Adjectives

anxious about bored with frightened of interested in kind to proud of responsible for similar to skilled at

Verbs

complain about disagree with pay for remind you of think about wait for

3 **For questions 1–8, read the text below and think of the preposition which best fits each gap. Use one word in each gap.**

Fun things for free!

Are you short (0) ...of... money? Don't worry (1) .... it! You can still have plenty of fun. Check out our list of fun activities that cost very little to do!

- Don't stay at home to eat your lunch. Escape your routine and take your lunch to the park as a picnic. You'll be surprised **(2)** .... the difference it makes.
- Be kind **(3)** .... your neighbours. Take their dog out for a long walk.

- Go and watch the sunset. It's good **(4)** .... your soul.
- Play some old Nintendo games online for free. They are just right for playing **(5)** .... friends.
- Are you interested **(6)** .... learning something new? Learn a card trick from YouTube and impress your friends.
- Or maybe you feel **(7)** .... a bit of culture? Find out what's on for free at your local museum or borrow a book **(8)** .... a friend.

4 **Write a prompt sheet of five examples of *adjective/verb + preposition* you want to remember from exercises 1–3.**

5 **Work in groups of four. Imagine you have all met at a party. Start up a conversation. Try to use your five phrases in the conversation as naturally as possible! Stop the conversation after <u>five minutes</u>. Can your classmates remember any of the adjectives or verbs you used?**

Exam tip!

Adjective / Verb + preposition *are common in the Part 2 task. Make a note of any new combinations and use them whenever you can!*

Pick a card!

1 **Play the card game.**

- **Work in groups of four and divide into Pair 1 and Pair 2. Place the eight question cards face down in the middle.**
- **Pair 1 picks up a card and reads the questions to Pair 2. Pair 2 chooses the correct answer (A or B) for each question and follows the path on the chart to find the correct playing card. They check the answer with Pair 1. If they have the correct answer, they keep the question card.**
- **Then Pair 2 picks up the next card from the pile and asks the questions.**

The pair who collects the most cards is the winner.

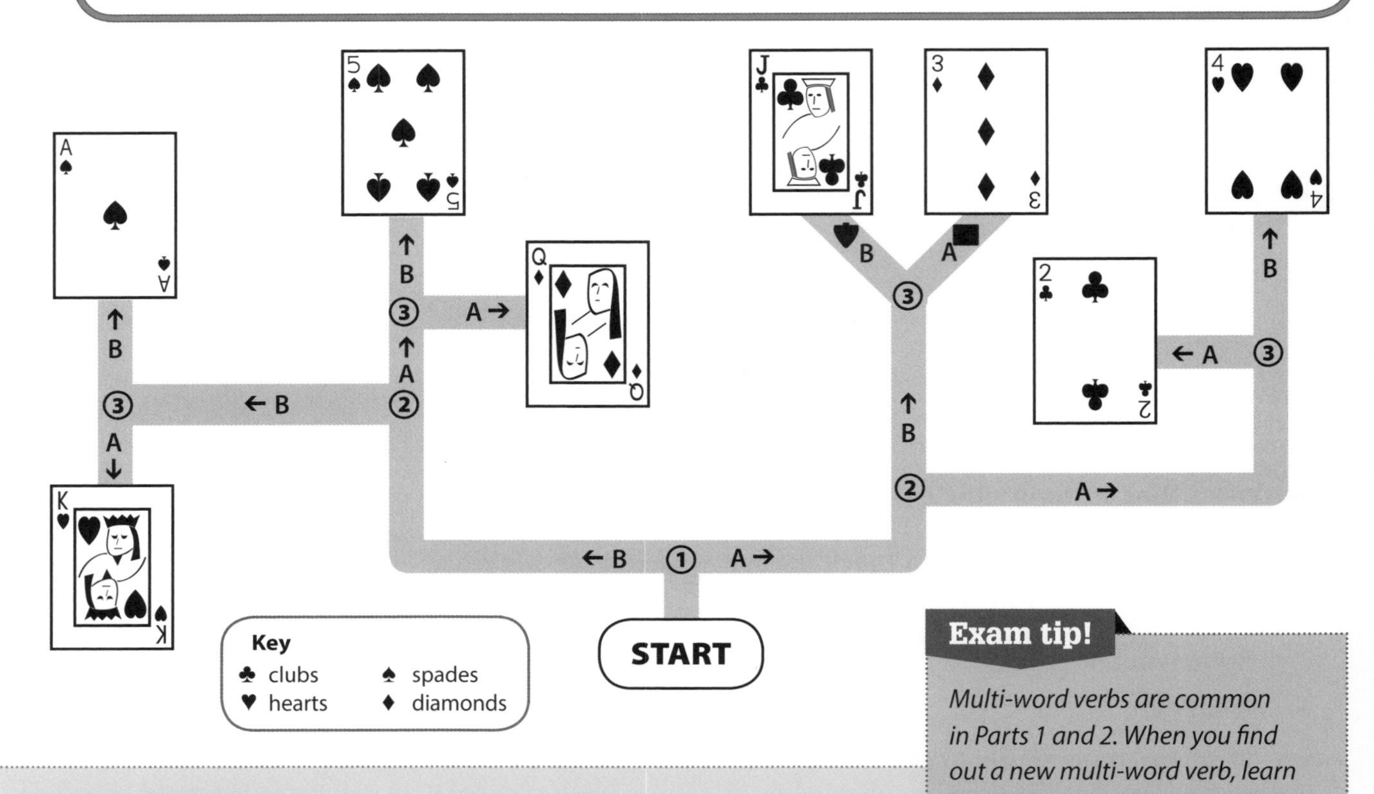

Exam tip!

Multi-word verbs are common in Parts 1 and 2. When you find out a new multi-word verb, learn an example sentence to help you remember how to use it.

EXAM TASK

2 **For questions 1–8, read the text below and think of the word which best fits each gap. Use one word in each gap.**

Starting a conversation

We all love catching **(0)** ......*up*...... with friends, but do you find it hard to **(1)** .... on with people you don't know? Is meeting new people something you don't look forward **(2)** .... ? The good news is it's a skill you can pick **(3)** .... , so read on for our top tips.

If you're at a party, hang **(4)** .... near the food table. This is not so you can eat everything there, but because nearly everybody comes to the food table at some point! Try chatting about something you **(5)** .... really into and invite others to do the same. If someone asks, 'How are you?' give them a full answer. Tell them what you've been doing and find **(6)** .... if they have the same interests. But be wary of **(7)** .... on and on about your favourite subject. If your plate is still piled up **(8)** .... food when everyone else has finished, you're probably talking too much!

Question cards

A

1 You are about to go into a meeting, but your colleague is still eating his lunch. What do you say?

A Eat up!
B Eat out!

2 It's been a long time since you've seen a good friend of yours. You send him a text. It says:

A Let's catch on!
B Let's catch up!

3 Your son is making very good progress at school. What do you say?

A Keep it on!
B Keep it up!

ANSWER: 1A, 2B, 3B: Jack of clubs

B

1 A project you're working on is taking you a very long time. What do you say?

A I'm getting at it.
B I'm getting through it.

2 You're describing your best friend to your aunt. What do you say?

A We get up really well.
B We get on really well.

3 You don't know whether to accept a job you've been offered. You decide to see a friend and

A talk it up.
B talk it over.

ANSWER: 1B, 2B, 3B: Ace of spades

C

1 You're listening to someone giving a presentation, but they have a very quiet voice. What do you say?

A Speak up, please!
B Speak across, please!

2 You're on holiday in Brazil. Someone asks you if you speak Portuguese. What do you say?

A I've picked up a few words.
B I've picked over a few words.

3 You've just heard a new band for the first time. And you love them. What do you say?

A I'm really into this.
B I'm really out of this.

ANSWER: 1A, 2A, 3A: two of clubs

D

1 Your friend asks you what you learnt on a guided tour but you don't remember very much. What do you say?

A I didn't take it in.
B I didn't take it off.

2 You've got an interview in the morning. You're meeting some friends tonight. What does your flatmate say to you?

A Don't stay in!
B Don't stay out late!

3 Your neighbour has been telling you every detail about his last round of golf. You're not keen on golf. You tell your friends about it. What do you say?

A He went on and on!
B He went up and up!

ANSWER: 1A, 2B, 3A: three of diamonds

Question cards

E

1 Your younger brother is not good at sharing. You try to explain why it's important but he doesn't seem to understand. What do you say to a friend?

A I can't get in to him.
B I can't get through to him.

2 You've met a new friend. You were friends from the first moment you met. What do you say?

A We just hit it off.
B We just hit it out.

3 You go to a party with a cousin. Your cousin wasn't keen to go, but you persuaded her. What do you tell your friends?

A I talked her out of it.
B I talked her into it.

ANSWER: 1B, 2A, 3B: five of spades

F

1 You're at the cinema and you meet a friend you haven't seen for a long time. You tell your colleagues about it. What do you say?

A I ran over Tim yesterday.
B I ran into Tim yesterday.

2 You've got three writing tasks to do as well as a practice test. What do you say to your friend?

A It's all piling up.
B It's all piling on.

3 You are offered a Saturday job, but you say no because the boss spoke to you as if you were a child. Your friend asked you what happened. What do you say?

A She really talked down to me.
B She really talked it up.

ANSWER: 1B, 2A, 3A: Queen of diamonds

G

1 Your music is on too loud. What does your sister say?

A Turn it down!
B Turn it away!

2 Your friend goes running every day. You decide to join him but it's tough. What do you say?

A I can't keep up!
B I can't keep out!

3 You want to talk to your gran but the phone line is busy. What do you say?

A I can't get on!
B I can't get through!

ANSWER: 1A, 2A, 3B: four of hearts

H

1 You're going on holiday with your cousins tomorrow but you don't know what time you're leaving. What do you ask?

A What time do we set up?
B What time do we set off?

2 You have some free time this weekend. What do you do?

A Hang on with friends.
B Hang out with friends.

3 Your friend is having a party. It should be good. What do you say?

A I'm looking forward to it.
B I'm looking out for it.

ANSWER: 1B, 2B, 3A: King of hearts

So you want to be a fashion designer …

1 **Read this interview with Matthew Harding, a successful young fashion designer from London. There is one word missing in each of Matthew's sentences. Insert the missing words.**

How long have you been designing?

a I've always *been* quite artistic but I began designing clothes when I went to art college.

Did you always want to go into fashion?

b No, it was my ambition when I was at school. I wanted to study psychology!

So who or what made you choose fashion?

c My tutor because he told me not get interested in fashion!

d When he told me it would be too difficult, I absolutely determined to do it!

Matthew Harding

What advice would you give to students who want to go into fashion?

e If you go into fashion because you love clothes and shopping, you probably not do that well.

f To succeed, you be desperate to create something.

g I think about fashion the time – I never stop.

h Be prepared to work for free or on very low pay for a number years.

i Success happens by chance, so you will definitely have to work very hard for it.

j Don't settle for anything but the best, and that includes to a really good fashion school.

2 **Compare your answers in pairs. Some of the items which are commonly tested in Part 2 of the exam are listed below. Match each of the items with the missing words from exercise 1.**

a) Auxiliary verbs
b) Participle forms of verbs
c) Modal verbs
d) Verb patterns *(verb + infinitive / gerund)*
e) Negative forms
f) Quantifiers

EXAM TASK

3 **For questions 1–8 read the text about London Fashion Week and think of the word that best fits each gap. Use one word in each gap.**

London Fashion Week takes place in London **(0)** ....*twice*.... each year, in February and September. It was first **(1)** .... in 1984 and now ranks alongside New York, Milan and Paris as one of the most influential fashion shows in the world.

Levi Palmer, who grew up in America before **(2)** .... to London, and British designer Matthew Harding are **(3)** .... strangers to London Fashion Week. The pair have **(4)**.................... presenting collections together at the show since 2011. The palmer//harding show in February 2015 used a total of 21 models, but **(5)** .... run smoothly, the event required 85 people – from hairdressers to security. Fashion shows are famous for their parties and celebrities, but designing a collection **(6)** .... be exhausting. So what **(7)** .... Levi Palmer do once it's all over? 'I'll get an Indian take away, flip through the hashtags on Instagram and go to bed! It's not glamorous at **(8)** .... !'

4 **Choose a short text about something you are interested in. Choose one of the categories from the list in exercise 2. Highlight all the examples of this in the text.**

Walking on air

1 **Work in pairs. Look at the photos. What do a BMX bike, a high wire and a bull have in common?**

2 **Read the texts about these sports. Some of the adjective forms are incorrect. Find and correct them.**

BMX RACING

BMX racing started in the early 1970s in southern California. This form of off-road racing on bikes is now one of the most ~~well-knowing~~ *well-known* extreme sports. There are many internationally events for the, often teenager, participants and unsurprisingly, it is fiercely competition. For those who say the sport is not extreme enough, there is the challenge of performing stunts. Judging by the injuries at the end of each competition, this sport is definitely extreme, always excited and definitely danger.

HIGHLINING

The extreme sport of highlining is becoming increasingly popularity, thanks to the drama images available online. To do this sport you need to be bravery, but also very athlete since you will be balancing on a nylon line less than an inch width which is suspended high above the ground. Highlining requires both physic and mental strength. Breathing and movements need to be control. 'Each and every move you make must be perfect. It's like walking on air,' says twenty-six-year-old professional, Jon Fait.

BULL RUNNING

Running away from an angrily bull is not everyone's idea of a fun activity, but for some thrill-seekers individuals, this sport is not to be missed. The bull-running festivals take place in a number of towns in Spain, Portugal and Mexico. The bull run in the Spanish city of Pamplona is world-famous. The bulls are led through the streets to the bull ring by runners. They run for 825 metres which usually takes about three or four terrified minutes. For those who don't want to be in the streets, amaze views of this very dangerous spectacle can be had from high up on the balconies of the houses in the old quarter.

Exam tip!

In the exam, you might have to form nouns, adjectives, verbs or adverbs. In this task, you only need adjectives.

EXAM TASK

3 **For questions 1–8, read the text below. Use the word given in capitals at the end of some of the lines to form an adjective that fits in the gap in the same line.**

Fans of James Bond films can get their kicks on a	
heli-skiing holiday. They might be **(0)** *disappointed*,	DISAPPOINTMENT
though, not to jump out of the helicopter, but to use	
a landing pad instead. And though the mountain	
slopes are **(1)** .... , the ski runs are tried and	SENSATION
tested. There are heli-skiing companies ready to take	
skiers out to the **(2)** .... wilderness in	SNOW
Canada, the USA and New Zealand. Skiers need to be **(3)** .... , but it's not necessary	SKILL
to be an ex-paratrooper. An **(4)** .... attitude and love of a challenge is a great start.	ENTHUSIASM
A heli-skiing holiday is not for the faint-hearted and it is **(5)** .... too. A holiday	EXPENSE
package can cost thousands of dollars, but the **(6)** .... reviews from skiers show that	WONDER
they consider it worth it.	
It is tempting to imagine that people who take part in extreme sports are **(7)**	ADVENTURE
loners, but participants on heli-skiing holidays are a **(8)** .... bunch, getting together	SOCIETY
and staying in touch to compare their incredible experiences.	

4 **Find examples of adjectives with each of these endings in exercises 2 and 3.**

-able / -ible	-ic	-ing
-ful	-ous	-y / -ly
-ive	-ed	-al

5 **There are many irregular forms too. How many adjectives can you find which do not fit into any of the groups above?**

....

....

Two cities

1 Read the text about Sydney. Underline words in the article that match the definitions a–f.

Ask someone to name the best five cities in the world and names like Perth, Adelaide, Melbourne and Sydney are unlikely to appear on the list. Yet these four underrated Australian cities frequently top polls for the best cities in the world to live in.

Sydney is a vibrant multicultural city with residents from countries as diverse as Vietnam, Lebanon and Italy. While many world cities like London are rapidly becoming overcrowded, Sydney enjoys a relatively low population of around five million. One of the drawbacks is the cost of housing. With prices increasing by over 30% in recent years, buying your own house is now unaffordable for many.

But a more beautiful city skyline than that of Sydney's harbour is impossible to imagine. So the few discontented residents can console themselves by watching the sun rise over the ocean on one of the city's 300 or so sunny days.

a) not possible

b) having too many people

c) not happy

d) be considered less good than it actually is

e) describes something that will probably not happen

f) too expensive

2 Discuss in pairs. What is the meaning of the prefix in each of these adjectives? What other prefixes are used in the text to mean the same as *un-*? Can you think of any others?

3 Play 'The prefix game'. Work in pairs: Student A and Student B.

EXAM TASK

4 For questions 1–8, read the text below. Use the word given in capitals at the end of some of the lines to form an adjective that fits in the gap in the same line.

New York City: the good and the bad

There are many reasons to love New York. One of the most ethnically diverse cities in the world – an **(0)** *unbelievable* 800 languages are spoken here – New York is at once the home of Broadway musicals and hip hop. And, of course, there's that **(1)** .... Manhattan skyline. But it's not all good. There are large and **(2)** .... variations in the standard of living across the city. An estimated 500,000 **(3)** .... immigrants work in New York without a permit. There has been some positive news: a decrease in the number of **(4)** .... people. However, nearly half the city's population still lives in near poverty – a far cry from the **(5)** .... and chic apartments in Manhattan. Average rents in some areas have risen by 75% and are now **(6)** .... for many. Workers in **(7)** .... jobs struggle to get by. A population increase in certain neighbourhoods has led to schools being **(8)** ....

(0) BELIEVABLE
(1) FORGETTABLE
(2) FAIR
(3) LEGAL
(4) EMPLOYED
(5) PRICED
(6) AFFORDABLE
(7) PAID
(8) CROWDED

THE PREFIX GAME

Student A

1 **Look at these words. Look up the meanings in your dictionary if you need to. Think of a context when these words could be used.**

dishonest, immature, irregular, overrated, overworked, unattractive, unforgettable, underpaid, understaffed

2 **Describe (but don't say!) your words to Student B. Can Student B guess the words?**

Example: *You don't tell the truth. (dishonest)*

3 **Student B will describe their words to you. Do you know the words? Use a prefix with one of the adjectives below to make the word.**

booked	excited	logical	certain	funded

obedient	developed	helpful	sensitive

THE PREFIX GAME

Student B

1 **Look at these words. Look up the meanings in your dictionary if you need to. Think of a context when these words could be used.**

disobedient, illogical, insensitive, overbooked, overexcited, uncertain, underfunded, unhelpful, underdeveloped

2 **Student A will describe their words to you. Use a prefix with one of the adjectives below to make the word.**

attractive	mature	regular	forgettable	paid

staffed	honest	rated	worked

3 **Describe (but don't say!) your words to Student A. Can Student A guess the words?**

Example: *You don't do as you are told. (disobedient)*

Making friends

1 Choose three of the questions. Tell a partner your answers. Discuss some of the other questions together.

What secret ability do you have?
On what occasions do you lie?
How would you describe happiness?
What qualities make a good friend?
What does maturity teach you?
What has been your greatest disappointment?
What is your best quality?
What side of your personality do you not like?
WHAT ADVICE WOULD YOU GIVE SOMEONE WHO IS STARTING A NEW RELATIONSHIP?

2 Change the adjectives to make nouns.

brilliant	....	hard	....	kind	....	patient	....
cheerful	....	honest	....	lonely	....	popular	....
confident	....	imaginative	....	loyal	....	selfish	....
disorganised	....	impatient	....	optimistic	....	wise	....
encourage	....	intelligent	....				

3 Make a list of the different noun endings you used in exercises 1 and 2.

Exam tip!

Watch out! Some nouns in Part 3 may be in the plural form.

EXAM TASK

4 Use the word given in capitals at the end of some of the lines to form a noun that fits in the gap in the same line.

How do children make friends?

Helping children understand about **(0)** *friendship* is one of the best things parents can do. FRIEND
Practise social **(1)** .... with your child, such as greeting a new friend, especially if your SKILLED
child lacks **(2)** .... One of the best ways for children to show they like someone is CONFIDENT
(3) .... When your children are young, you may find that they need lots of KIND
(4) .... to share but it is equally important they know when to stop. Otherwise they ENCOURAGE
may give away money or even favourite **(5)** .... BELONG
Even very young children show a **(6)** .... for one friend or another. Research shows PREFER
that children look for peers who have things in common. Sharing lots of fun **(7)** .... is ACTIVE
a great way for children to make friends. But a play date at home can be trickier for your child
than it sounds. Helping your child to behave in ways that another child enjoys and resolving
any **(8)** .... will need to be part of the fun! AGREE

5 Add nouns from exercise 4 to your lists. Are there any nouns that don't fit into any of the groups?

Word dice

1 Work in small groups and play the dice game. Each group needs a dice.

Game rules

1 Throw the dice. Look at the verb list below which matches the number. Choose a verb from the list.

2 Throw the dice again. Look at the instruction which matches this number. Follow the instruction for your verb. You can use a dictionary to help you.

anger	act	concern	choose	deepen	brighten
control	advise	doubt	demand	heighten	clean
frighten	behave	legalise	give	lengthen	darken
help	contrast	marry	introduce	shorten	die
know	practise	predict	lose	strengthen	empty
speak	produce	save	prove	weaken	like
think	vary	see	succeed	widen	live

Instructions

- (1) Say the verb with the correct pronunciation and stress.
- (2) Form a noun from this verb. Use it in a sentence.
- (3) Form an adjective from this verb. Use it in a sentence.
- (4) Cover up the verb. How many letters are in the verb?
- (5) Cover up the verb. Spell it backwards.
- (6) Form a noun or an adjective from this verb.

Exam tip!

Learn new words together with any other common words that can be formed from them.

EXAM TASK

2 For questions 1–8, read the text below. Use the word given in capitals at the end of some of the lines to form a word that fits in the gap in the same line.

The oldest **(0)** ......*known*...... dice are at least 8,000 years old. Early dice were quite basic and	**KNOW**
consisted of **(1)** .... objects that people had found, such as fruit stones, shells and	**NATURE**
pebbles. Many early cultures used dice. The Ancient Greeks made dice from the ankle bones of	
(2) .... hoofed animals. These dice had four faces and were probably used to make	**VARY**
(3) .... about the future.	**PREDICT**
Dice games were common in Roman times, despite not being **(4)** .... there. The Romans	**LAW**
brought the dice to the UK where they were an immediate **(5)** .... with peasants. These	**SUCCEED**
games were one of the few leisure **(6)** .... poor people could afford.	**ACTION**
When European settlers arrived in the USA in the seventeenth century, they brought dice games	
with them. In New Orleans, the **(7)** .... of a French game called *crapaud* was very popular	**INTRODUCE**
with slaves. They began to **(8)** .... the name to 'craps' and this is still one of the most	**SHORT**
popular dice games in the USA.	

Your turn!

Student A

1 Match the phrases in each column which have a similar meaning.

1	Don't forget!	**a)**	be bound to
2	I'm sorry!	**b)**	can't afford
3	still not	**c)**	remind
4	will almost certainly	**d)**	have no difficulty in
5	not have enough money	**e)**	apologise
6	find it easy to	**f)**	not yet

Exam tip!

In Part 4 of the exam, you can only write between two and five words.

2 For each of these sentences, write a second sentence which has a similar meaning, using the phrases (a–f) from exercise 1 to help you.

a) 'Don't forget to turn off the headlights!' he told me. *He reminded me to turn off the headlights.*

b) 'I'm sorry I didn't ring you before,' my sister said. ....

c) I still haven't filled in the form. ....

d) It'll almost certainly rain if we have the party outdoors! ....

e) I don't have enough money for a holiday this year. ....

f) They found it easy to find a buyer for their flat. ....

---

3 BE THE EXAMINER! Choose which word is best to have as the prompt in each of the sentences from exercise 2. Then write part of each sentence for Student B to complete. Remember they can only use between two and five words.

a) 'Don't forget to turn off the headlights!' he told me.

He .... *the headlights.* **REMINDED**

b) 'I'm sorry I didn't ring you before,' my sister said.

....

c) I still haven't filled in the form.

....

d) It'll almost certainly rain if we have the party outdoors!

....

e) I don't have enough money for a holiday this year.

....

f) They found it easy to find a buyer for their flat.

....

Student B

Exam tip!

In Part 4 of the exam, you can only write between two and five words.

1 Match the phrases from each column which have a similar meaning.

1 If I were you ...	**a)** must have
2 If only ...	**b)** took more time
3 so	**c)** such
4 I'm sure	**d)** never been so frightened
5 didn't finish	**e)** advise
6 was the most frightening	**f)** regret

2 For each of these sentences, write a second sentence which has a similar meaning, using the phrases (a–f) from exercise 1 to help you.

a) 'If I were you, I'd pack an extra jumper,' my cousin told me. *My cousin advised me to pack an extra jumper.*

b) 'If only I had spoken to him earlier,' I thought. ....

c) I didn't expect the bag to be so heavy. ....

d) I'm sure the manager was very angry when he found out. ....

e) They didn't finish the building work as early as I had hoped. ....

f) It was the most frightening thing I've ever done. ....

3 BE THE EXAMINER! **Choose which word is best to have as the prompt in each of the sentences from exercise 2. Then write part of each sentence for Student A to complete. Remember they can only use between two and five words.**

a) 'If I were you, I'd pack an extra jumper,' my cousin told me.

My cousin .... *an extra jumper.* ADVISED

b) 'If only I had spoken to him earlier,' I thought.

....

c) I didn't expect the bag to be so heavy.

....

d) I'm sure the manager was very angry when he found out.

....

e) They didn't finish the building work as early as I had hoped.

....

f) It was the most frightening thing I've ever done.

....

Earthquakes in Nepal

Student A

1 **Work in pairs. You have some sentences from a newspaper article about the 2015 earthquakes in Nepal. Take it in turns to tell your partner the sentences, but turn active sentences into passive sentences and direct speech into reported speech.**

1 Two earthquakes in Nepal have affected about a quarter of the population.

2 ....

....

3 The earthquake has destroyed entire villages.

4 ....

....

5 The earthquakes damaged a large number of ancient monuments in the capital, Kathmandu.

6 ....

....

7 People rescued a fifteen-year-old boy from the debris of a seven-storey building.

8 ....

....

9 Rescuers found a very old man under the rubble – people think he is 101.

10 ....

....

11 'It was pretty scary. Snow and rocks and houses started coming down,' said a tourist who was just north of the capital.

12 ....

....

Student B

1 **Work in pairs. You have some sentences from a newspaper article about the 2015 earthquakes in Nepal. Take it in turns to tell your partner the sentences, but turn active sentences into passive sentences and direct speech into reported speech.**

1 ....

....

2 On April 25 2015 a massive 7.8 magnitude earthquake hit Nepal.

3 ....

....

4 Just 17 days later a second quake followed the disaster.

5 ....

....

6 The quake made hundreds of thousands of people homeless.

7 ....

....

8 A medical worker said, 'It is miraculous. The boy was under the rubble for 120 hours.'

9 ....

....

10 A journalist at the scene said, 'He only suffered minor injuries.'

11 ....

....

12 A spokesperson from the Nepal Tourism Board told us, 'We hope the return of tourists will restore the lives of people here.'

2 **Compare your sentences with the newspaper article.**

Earthquakes in Nepal

About a quarter of the population has been affected by two earthquakes in Nepal.

On April 25 2015, Nepal was hit by a massive 7.8 magnitude earthquake. Entire villages have been destroyed. Just seventeen days later the disaster was followed by a second quake. A large number of ancient monuments in the capital, Kathmandu, were damaged. Hundreds of thousands of people were made homeless by the quake.

A fifteen-year-old boy was rescued from the debris of a seven-storey building. A medical worker said it was miraculous. The boy had been under the rubble for 120 hours.

A very old man was found under the rubble. He is thought to be 101. A journalist at the scene reported that he had only suffered minor injuries.

A tourist who was just north of the capital said the earthquake had been pretty scary. Snow and rocks and houses had started coming down.

A spokesperson from the Nepal Tourism Board told us that they hoped the return of tourists would restore the lives of people there.

EXAM TASK

3 **Sentences 1–6 are about the 1934 earthquake in Nepal. Complete the second sentence so that it has a similar meaning to the first sentence, using the word given. Do not change the word given. You must use between two and five words, including the word given.**

0 The earthquake was on January 15, 1934.

THAT

It was on January 15, 1934 ......*that the earthquake took*...... place.

1 Everyone says this was the worst earthquake in Nepalese history.

SAID

The earthquake .... the worst in Nepalese history.

2 People think that survivors gathered in large tents.

THOUGHT

Survivors .... in large tents.

3 There was serious damage to the Dharhara Tower in the 1934 quake too.

WAS

The Dharhara Tower .... in the 1934 quake.

4 The town of Birgunj needed rebuilding after the earthquake.

HAD

The town of Birgunj .... after the earthquake.

5 'I feel lucky to have survived two killer quakes,' 90-year-old Parsuram said to me.

TOLD

90-year-old Parsuram .... to have survived two killer quakes.

6 'The quake was scarier in 1934,' Parsuram also recalled.

BEING

Parsuram also remembered .... in 1934.

Notice this!

1 Have you seen notices similar to these before? Where might you find each one?

1 PATIENTS WITHOUT AN APPOINTMENT WILL NOT BE SEEN

2

3

4

5 YOU WILL NEED TO SHOW A VALID FORM OF ID TO COLLECT YOUR ORDER

6 **CUSTOMERS** THERE IS AN OPTIONAL 10% SERVICE CHARGE

7 It is advisable to take out insurance before you travel.

8 ALL STUDENTS WHO ARRIVE AFTER 8.45 MUST SIGN THE LATE BOOK.

2 For each of the signs above, write two sentences with a similar meaning, using the word given. Do not change the word given. You must use between two and five words, including the word given.

1 a) Patients without an appointment ......*can't be seen*...... by a doctor. **(can't)**

b) Patients with no appointment .... a doctor. **(able)**

2 a) .... use the beach. **(must)**

b) .... on the beach. **(allowed)**

3 a) Applications .... received by 10th July. **(to)**

b) It .... your application by 10th July. **(necessary)**

4 a) The council .... park here. **(let)**

b) You .... here. **(permitted)**

5 a) A valid form of ID .... your order. **(required)**

b) You .... valid form of ID when you collect your order. **(have)**

6 a) Customers .... a 10% tip if they want to. **(can)**

b) Customers .... a 10% tip. **(have)**

7 a) You .... before the trip. **(should)**

b) You .... without insurance. **(ought)**

8 a) Students who arrive after 8.45........................ the late book. **(will)**

b) It .... who arrive after 8.45 sign the late book. **(essential)**

Exam tip!

In Part 4, contractions count as two words. 'Can't' is one word as it is a contraction of 'cannot'.

Hedgehogs and bats

1 **Work in pairs. Choose a synonym from the box to replace the underlined words in the text.**

☐ broken up	a catch sight of	☐ cope with	☐ going down	☐ die out
☐ make up	☐ on the look-out	☐ run over	☐ take care of	☐ take part in

Hedgehogs in danger of extinction

It's always been rare to **(a)** <u>see</u> a hedgehog in the daytime, but the nocturnal ramblings that take them through our gardens **(b)** <u>searching</u> for worms, slugs and snails are also on the decrease. Numbers of UK hedgehogs are **(c)** <u>declining</u> at the same rate as tigers. If nothing is done to **(d)** <u>look after</u> our prickly friends, ecologists believe that it is inevitable that hedgehogs will **(e)** <u>become extinct</u>. One reason for the decline is the use of pesticides which kill off the invertebrates that **(f)** <u>form</u> most of their diet. In addition to this, hedgehogs are having to **(g)** <u>deal with</u> habitat fragmentation. Hedgehogs look for food over a wide area but their habitats are being **(h)** <u>divided</u> by garden fences and roads. Roads pose an additional risk. Many hedgehogs are **(i)** <u>killed by vehicles</u> on roads. Wildlife lovers in the UK are being encouraged to **(j)** <u>participate in</u> hedgehog conservation programmes.

EXAM TASK

2 **Complete the second sentence so that it has a similar meaning to the first sentence, using the word given. Do not change the word given. You must use between two and five words, including the word given.**

0 Many people take no notice of the bats in our summer skies.
PAY
Many people *do not pay attention to* the bats in our summer skies.

1 It is unfair that bats are disapproved of by some people.
LOOK
It is unfair that some people .... bats.

2 Some bats are on the decline because there are not enough roost sites.
RUN
Some bats are on the decline because they are starting .... roost sites.

3 In fact, bats are tolerated in some buildings.
UP
In fact many people .... bats in some buildings.

4 I recently decided to build a bat box to put in my shed.
MIND
I recently made .... a bat box to put in my shed.

5 Bats may take some time to use the box.
MAKE
It may take some time before .... box.

Exam tip!
When you come across a new multi-word verb or idiom, learn a synonym for it at the same time.

Reading between the lines

1 Look at these phrases containing the word *read*. Match the underlined parts of the sentences with their definitions a–f.

1. I'm having to read between the lines here.
2. You can read me like a book!
3. You can take it as read that we support you.
4. It was an odd thing to say, but try not to read too much into it!
5. This is his first novel and it reads well.
6. That was a fantastic read.

a) know someone so well that you know how they are feeling
b) be written in a skilled and appealing way
c) believe that an action or remark has some special importance (which is often not true)
d) understand what someone means even when they do not tell you directly
e) a very enjoyable book or story
f) assume something is true without discussing it further

2a Look at the photo of Bridget Jones below. What do you think she is like?

2b Read the extract from *Bridget Jones's Diary* by Helen Fielding. Apart from Bridget and her mother, how many different people are mentioned in the extract?

Exam tip!

Some of the questions in Part 5 will test how well you can read between the lines and understand what is implied by the writer.

***Bridget Jones's Diary* was partly based on *Pride and Prejudice* by Jane Austen. It was made into a very successful film starring Renée Zellweger as Bridget.**

3 Work in pairs. Discuss the answers to the following questions.

a) Is Bridget looking forward to the New Year's Day party? How do we know this?
b) Does Bridget enjoy the conversation with her mother? What words and phrases tell us this?
c) How would you describe Bridget's mother?

4 BE THE EXAMINER! Complete the two questions below with words from the text. Give them to a classmate to answer.

Example: *What does the word 'desperately' in line 33 tell us about how Bridget is feeling?*

a) What does the word / phrase '.................................' in line .... tell us about ....?
b) What does the word / phrase '.................................' suggest about ....?

Sunday 1 January

Noon. London: my flat. The last thing on earth I feel physically, emotionally or mentally equipped to do is drive to Una and Geoffrey Alconbury's New Year's Day Turkey Curry Buffet in Grafton Underwood. Geoffrey and Una Alconbury are my parents' best friends and, as Uncle Geoffrey never tires of reminding me, have known me since I was running round the lawn with no clothes on. My mother rang up at 8.30 in the morning last August Bank Holiday and forced me to promise to go. She approached it via a cunningly circuitous route.

'Oh, hello, darling. I was just ringing to see what you wanted for Christmas.'

'Christmas?'

'Would you like a surprise, darling?'

'No!' I bellowed. 'Sorry. I mean…'

'I wondered if you'd like a set of wheels for your suitcase.'

'But I haven't got a suitcase.'

'Why don't I get you a little suitcase with wheels attached. You know, like air hostesses have.'

'I've already got a bag.'

'Oh, darling, you can't go around with that tatty green canvas thing. You look like some sort of Mary Poppins person who's fallen on hard times. Just a little compact case with a pull-out handle. It's amazing how much you can get in. Do you want it in navy on red or red on navy?'

'Mum. It's eight thirty in the morning. It's summer. It's very hot. I don't want an air hostess bag.'

'Julie Enderby's got one. She says she never uses anything else.'

'Who's Julie Enderby?'

'You know *Julie*, darling! Mavis Enderby's daughter, Julie! The one that's got that super-dooper job at Arthur Andersen…'

'Mum…'

'Always takes it on her trips…'

'I don't want a little bag with wheels on.'

'I'll tell you what. Why don't Jamie, Daddy and I all club together and get you a proper new big suitcase *and* a set of wheels?'

Exhausted, I held the phone away from my ear, puzzling about where the missionary luggage-Christmas-gift zeal had stemmed from. When I put the phone back she was saying: '...in actual fact, you can get them with a compartment with bottles for your bubble bath and things. The other thing I thought of was a shopping trolley.'

line 33 'Is there anything you'd like for Christmas?' I said desperately, blinking in the dazzling Bank Holiday sunlight.

'No, no,' she said airily. 'I've got everything I need. Now, darling,' she suddenly hissed, 'you will be coming to Geoffrey and Una's New Year's Day Turkey Curry Buffet this year, won't you?'

'Ah. Actually, I…' I panicked wildly. What could I pretend to be doing? '…think I might have to work on New Year's Day.'

'That doesn't matter. You can drive up after work. Oh, did I mention? Malcolm and Elaine Darcy are coming and bringing Mark with them. Do you remember Mark, darling? He's one of those top-notch barristers. Masses of money. Divorced. It doesn't start till eight.'

Oh God. Not another strangely dressed opera freak with bushy hair burgeoning from a side-parting. 'Mum, I've told you. I don't need to be fixed up with…'

'Now come along, darling. Una and Geoffrey have been holding the New Year buffet since you were running round the lawn with no clothes on! Of course you're going to come. And you'll be able to use your new suitcase.'

Extract from 'Bridget Jones's Diary' by Helen Fielding

5 **Look at these five exam-style questions. In pairs or small groups match each question with a set of multiple-choice answers. Choose the correct answer from the four options. Discuss why the other answers are not correct.**

a) How does Bridget feel about her decision to go to the party?

b) What does Bridget suggest is her mother's reason for phoning her?

c) What does Bridget's mother want her to know about Mark?

d) Why does Bridget suspect that her mother has mentioned Mark?

e) What does the phrase 'cunningly circuitous route' in line 6 tell us about Bridget's mother?

1

A He has a suitcase with wheels attached.

B He goes to the opera.

C He is rich and is no longer married

D He is a friend of a friend.

2

A She has bad memories of the party's hosts.

B She is not looking forward to using her new suitcase.

C She will find it difficult to go to the party because she is working.

D She has not been left with any choice in the matter.

3

A She talks a lot about unimportant matters.

B She can be clever and not always honest.

C She doesn't have a very organised social life.

D She is frustrated by her daughter's attitude.

4

A She hopes Mark and Bridget will start a relationship.

B She wants him to buy Bridget an expensive Christmas present.

C She expects he will get Bridget a new job.

D She wants to meet Mark's parents.

5

A She asks for her advice on buying a suitcase.

B She invites her to a New Year's party.

C She gives her news about a friend.

D She's hoping to find out what Bridget wants for Christmas.

Kevin's secret

1 Read the text about Kevin Liu. What do you find surprising about Kevin's story?

When Kevin Liu was at primary school, he didn't realise how good he had it. He was living with his mum, dad and younger brother Ka-ren, in a small rented apartment in the Chinatown neighbourhood of Manhattan in New York City. The apartment was above his parents' grocery store, which also had a few arcade games for kids to play on. Ka-ren and Kevin weren't allowed to eat the sweets in the shop or join in the arcade games, but their parents did let them help out. The brothers enjoyed counting out the customers' change. Though his parents didn't own the shop, it was still home. Kevin never really thought about whether he was happy, it was just the way his life was. (1)

Everything changed for Kevin and his family when Kevin was in his last year at Primary School. Kevin's family did not know their landlord very well, but he owned a lot of places in the area. When Kevin got home from school one day, the landlord told him and his family to gather all their belongings, then he kicked them out without the slightest explanation or even any notice. The family lost their business and their home all at once. The family had no choice but to move to the Life Family Shelter, a temporary homeless shelter in lower Manhattan. (2)

Kevin didn't fully understand what was happening at first, but after a few weeks, it finally sank in: he and his family were homeless. It was humiliating and humbling. Kevin didn't tell anyone at school what was going on at this time. If anyone ever asked him where he lived, he would be really vague. As time went on, he started to lie outright. He felt he could never truly be himself and open up to friends because he always carried this secret around with him. It was a lonely time. (3)

Kevin and his family had a private room to sleep in at the shelter, which housed ninety families, but it was a quarter of the size or their old living space and cramped with bunk beds against the wall. They shared a bathroom with everyone else on their floor. Some of the other kids at the shelter would mess about and turn off the shower light when Kevin was in there. The only good part about living in the shelter was that Kevin got to go to an after-school programme that was run by a homeless charity. It was a quiet place where Kevin could do his homework or play music. Kevin heaved a sigh of relief whenever he got to the after-school programme. It was an escape from the noise of the hot, overcrowded shelter he shared with people he didn't know. (4)

After three long years, Kevin's parent finally found affordable housing. They had two bedrooms, their own bathroom and a kitchen where they could cook their own food. Kevin was so excited about moving out of the shelter. He was desperate to have his own space again. 'It's funny,' he says. 'You don't realise how much you appreciate stuff until you're forced to live without it. Now everything feels luxurious!' 

When Kevin turned 17 in April this year, he started feeling different about his experience. For the first time, he didn't feel ashamed. He decided that it was time to tell someone, so he told his friend, Jason. Kevin was unsure how to broach the subject and was worried Jason would turn his back on him, but he was determined to try. 'Jason couldn't really believe I had kept it a secret from him so long,' Kevin told me, 'but he was awesome about it.' Jason was supportive and didn't treat Kevin any differently because of his past. The whole conversation went so well that Kevin felt confident enough to tell other friends too. Kevin has also started volunteering at the after-school club. He wants to help other kids that are going through the same thing as he did. Sometimes he helps them with their homework or plays basketball with them. He tells them how he'd like to go to college someday or try to become an actor. 'I hope they look at me and see how well I'm doing now,' Kevin told me with a smile. 'I want them to think: *I can do that too!*' 

2 **Work in pairs. Find the sections of the text that contain the answers to these questions and highlight each part.**

a) What impression do we get of Kevin's parents?

b) What is the writer's attitude towards the landlord?

c) Kevin didn't tell anyone at primary school what had happened because …

d) What is meant by the phrase 'heaved a sigh of relief'?

e) How does Kevin feel when he moves out of the shelter?

f) How did Kevin feel about speaking to Jason?

3 **Read your highlighted sections through again. Predict the kind of answer you are expecting for each of the questions in exercise 2.**

4 **Now do the exam task on page 37.**

5 **Answer the question below and discuss in your pairs. Do you think Kevin is successful in his aim?**

In this article Kevin wants us to know that

A we should work hard to be able to afford what we want in life.

B circumstances like these will never happen to us.

C we should never assume we can have everything we need.

D homelessness can happen to anyone.

6 **What do you think? Choose the correct answers.**

1 For Part 5 of the exam, it is a good idea to

A read the text once and then try to answer the questions.

B answer the questions without looking back at the text.

C read the relevant sections of the text again before trying to answer the questions.

D throw your hands in the air and move on to Part 6.

2 One way of approaching the task is to

A read each question first and decide what the answer will be.

B read each question first and predict what the answer will be.

C read the options without reading the question.

D choose the answers you like best.

3 When you look at the multiple-choice answers to a question,

A circle the one you think is correct and cross out the others without reading them.

B circle the one you think is correct and read the other options quickly.

C choose the one which matches the text and think about why the other answers are not correct.

D close your eyes and pick an answer.

Exam tip!

In Part 5, the final multiple-choice question may focus on the overall theme or purpose of the text.

EXAM TASK

You are going to read a magazine article about a young boy called Kevin whose family fell upon hard times. For questions 1–6, choose the answer (A, B, C or D) which you think fits best according to the text.

1 What impression do we get of Kevin's parents?

A They are not particularly hard-working.
B They are fairly strict with their children.
C They wish they could afford to buy their own home.
D They think Kevin should be thankful for the standard of living he has.

2 What is the writer's attitude towards the landlord?

A She thinks the landlord acted reasonably towards Kevin and his family.
B She suggests the landlord showed some sympathy for Kevin's parents.
C She is critical of the fact that the landlord gave them no warning.
D She believes landlords have too many properties.

3 Kevin didn't tell anyone at primary school what had happened because

A he had a tendency to tell lies.
B he didn't often confide in his friends.
C he was confused by what was happening to him.
D he was embarrassed by being homeless.

4 What is meant by the phrase 'heaved a sigh of relief' in line 47?

A breathed heavily
B felt surprised
C was exhausted
D felt calmer

5 How does Kevin feel when he moves out of the shelter?

A He is anxious because the new housing is expensive.
B He realises he has missed his privacy.
C He is pleased because he will be able to concentrate better on his homework.
D He considers that life at the shelter was better than he realised at the time.

6 How did Kevin feel about speaking to Jason?

A worried that the conversation would affect their friendship
B concerned because he knew that Jason didn't like people having secrets
C anxious that Jason would ask him to volunteer at the after-school club
D resigned to the fact that Jason would reveal Kevin's secret to other friends

A new Golden Age?

1 Look at the phrases. Group them according to the emotion they express. Write A for annoyed, E for embarrassed or W for worried.

a) He got butterflies in his stomach before the show. ☐

b) It's so irritating. ☐

c) She had misgivings about letting her daughter walk home on her own. ☐

d) That's really getting on my nerves. ☐

e) I felt a bit sheepish about arriving late. ☐

f) It's starting to bother me. A

g) Being alone always makes him anxious. ☐

h) All the attention made her feel awkward. ☐

i) I felt humiliated when they laughed at me. ☐

j) The teacher's comments made me cross. ☐

k) He went red in the face. ☐

l) She felt uneasy about the situation. ☐

COMIC BOOKS: A NEW GOLDEN AGE?

Sales of comic books are at an all-time high and the rising trend looks set to continue. Comics have always been a popular genre so what has caused this sudden surge in interest?

The Fantastic Four from Marvel Comics

The comic book as we know it really started in 1938 with the introduction of 'Superman' in Action Comics #1. Up until then, comic books were really only collections of comic strips that had already appeared in the newspapers. The book was a smash hit and began what's known as the Golden Age of comic books. The stories of heroes with superhuman powers, secret identities and memorable outfits – think Batman, Captain Marvel and Captain America – were read by millions every week. While many of the heroes were men, there were heroines too. Wonder Woman first appeared in 1941. Sales of the inspirational stories of heroes who triumphed over evil increased during World War II. In the USA, the patriotic Captain America was especially in demand.

Though the superhero comics were the top sellers, other genres also appeared during the Golden Age. Animal stories and science fiction were in favour, as were crime stories, in particular The Spirit, a masked detective who captured villains. After the war, crime and horror became a regular theme and parents started to have misgivings about their children reading them. It wasn't long before comic books suffered a backlash as psychologists claimed they were bad for children.

Even back in 1938, there were adults who read comic books, but they were probably a bit embarrassed about it. But things changed in the 1960s with the emergence of the more modern superhero. It all started with Marvel Comics' Fantastic Four series, by Stan Lee and Jack Kirby, aimed at teenagers and college students. Unlike the popular but now rather tired heroes of DC Comics, Marvel's new heroes were real-life. The Fantastic Four were like a dysfunctional but loving family who got on each other's nerves and had the same faults as the rest of us. Spider-Man was a teenager who had to revise for exams and pluck up the courage to talk to girls. Comic book readers found plenty they could relate to.

In the 1980s came the graphic novel. A graphic novel is a collection of several comic book issues or an extended story, bound like a paperback book, or, as comic book author Neil Gaiman puts it, 'a fat comic that can be sold as a book in a bookstore'. The audience for graphic novels has increased because they can be mass-marketed and shipped to bookstores, not just comic book specialists. In the digital era, graphic novels also lend themselves to being read on tablets such as iPads and even smartphones. Digital platforms are a good entry point for readers who are discovering graphic novels for the first time. Interestingly, an increasing number of these new buyers are women and girls.

The success of the Hollywood movies *X-Men* (2000) and *Spider-Man* (2002) has started a love affair between Hollywood and the graphic novel. Films like the Iron Man series and The Avengers are some of the highest grossing films of all time. Graphic novel expert Stephen Weiner believes that, thanks to Hollywood, no one need feel sheepish about reading a graphic novel on their way home any more. 'The big success of *Spider-Man* and *X-Men* really changed it,' he says. 'They were able to take the mythical metaphors and give them human drama for people who didn't read comics.' And many of those people now do read comics.

Exam tip!

In Part 5, some of the questions focus on the feelings of the writer or people mentioned in the text. Learn groups of phrases which are associated with particular emotions.

EXAM TASK

2 **First read the article about comic books. For questions 1–6, choose the answer (A, B, C or D) which you think fits best according to the text.**

1 The words 'a smash hit' in line 4 tells us that Superman was
A a disappointment.
B a bestseller.
C a trendsetter.
D a bargain.

2 Which of these is true about comic books in the post-war years?
A Parents were uneasy about their effect on children.
B Comic book stories were being read by many psychologists.
C Only comics featuring superheroes sold well.
D The popularity of comics continued to rise.

3 What does the writer suggest about modern superheroes?
A They are boring and rather predictable.
B They are often irritated with each other.
C They have similar character traits to their readers.
D They don't get on with girls.

4 What do we find out about graphic novels in the fourth paragraph?
A Women now make up a large percentage of the readers.
B They are more easily available than before.
C They are better if read on smartphones and tablets.
D They are not popular with comic book writers.

5 What does the writer suggest is one of the greatest advantages of the crossover between graphic novels and Hollywood?
A Readers don't need to feel awkward reading a graphic novel.
B Authors of graphic novels can achieve worldwide success.
C Film companies make a great deal of money.
D There are likely to be more films made from graphic novels.

6 What is the writer's purpose in writing this article?
A A criticism of the effects of the genre on teenagers.
B An analysis of the increasing influence of graphic novels on other media.
C A justification of why reading comics is an acceptable pastime.
D An explanation of the development and success of the graphic novel.

3 **Which of the phrases from exercise 1 are used in the article and multiple-choice questions?**

Nowhere boy

1 John Lennon was a member of The Beatles, a hugely successful British band from Liverpool. Read the extract from the story of his childhood based on the film *Nowhere Boy*. Who do you think Mimi was?

John glanced up at the clock. He knew his friend Pete would be waiting outside the house. Every day before school, Pete came to call for him on his bike. As John pushed his own bicycle out, he heard a knock from the front window. He knew why. Every day, they went through the same thing. He turned to see Mimi standing there, making circles with her fingers and thumbs and holding them up to her eyes.

'Glasses, John!' she shouted.

'Glasses, John!' repeated Pete with a laugh.

line 8 John sighed. He took his glasses out of his pocket and reluctantly put them on. As soon as they were round the next corner, he took his glasses off again. He wondered if Mimi knew that.

Outside the house, John was a different person. He was always ready with a joke, and if it bothered him that he hurt someone's feelings he didn't show it. As he and Pete cycled on, they rode past three older boys from their school. One of them was taller and heavier than his two friends.

'Oy, you!' John shouted to him. 'Keep out of the chip shop!'

The older boy shouted something angrily back.

'He thinks he's tough!' said Pete with a laugh.

'Who cares?' said John. John pedalled faster, laughing as he went, but he glanced over his shoulder at the boy, just in case.

John rarely paid attention in class. He spent his time drawing cartoons in his exercise books. John knew that his behaviour was a distraction for the class, but he couldn't stop himself.

The headmaster, Mr Pobjoy, looked at John coldly. He had seen more of John Lennon recently that he would have liked. The wiry young lad stood in front of him, full of impatient energy.

'You'll be lucky if you get a job in the docks,' Mr Pobjoy told John. 'You're going nowhere.'

John knew what Mr Pobjoy wanted. He was hoping that John would say sorry and promise to try harder in future. But that wasn't John's style. Instead, he looked the headmaster right in the eye. 'Is nowhere full of geniuses, sir? Because if it is, I probably belong there.'

That evening Mimi sat alone in the sitting room, a cigarette in one hand and a book in the other. The sound of Tchaikovsky on the radio filled the room. Laughter came from the stairs as John and his uncle, George, joked together. John and George were putting a speaker up on the wall in John's room so that he could hear the radio from downstairs in his own bedroom. Mimi didn't join them; she didn't even look up from her book.

Finally, John pressed the button upstairs and the sound of Tchaikovsky filled his room.

'Mimi! It works!' John shouted as he ran to the top of the stairs. 'Can we see if something else is on?' He wanted some music to match his excitement.

Nothing or no one was going to get in the way of Mimi's enjoyment of the classical music.

'No, John. We do not turn Tchaikovsky over,' she answered. Another rule of the house. She sounded as if she was explaining something very obvious to a little child. But John was enjoying himself too much to let it worry him. He rushed back to his room and leapt onto his bed. His uncle smiled wanly at John's enthusiasm, but John was oblivious to how tired his uncle was looking.

2 **Work in pairs. Underline words in the extract with similar meanings to the following words or phrases. You have <u>three minutes</u>.**

a) looked quickly

b) said again

c) if he minded

d) strong and aggressive

e) something that stops you paying attention

f) fortunate

g) prevent

h) unaware

EXAM TASK

3 **For questions 1–6, choose the answer (A, B, C or D) which you think fits best according to the text.**

Exam tip!

Underline words in the multiple choice options with similar meanings to words in the text.

1 In line 8, what does 'reluctantly' mean?
- **A** impatiently
- **B** in a hurry
- **C** happily
- **D** unwillingly

2 By saying that John is 'going nowhere' the headmaster implies that John is not going to …
- **A** achieve success.
- **B** see the world.
- **C** leave the headmaster's office.
- **D** be content.

3 What is John's attitude towards the headmaster?
- **A** He wants Mr Pobjoy to think well of him.
- **B** He is apologetic for his actions.
- **C** He shows him little respect.
- **D** He is uninterested in what he has to say.

4 What does the writer suggest about John's behaviour at school?
- **A** He is aggressive towards others.
- **B** He doesn't care what anyone thinks.
- **C** He enjoys getting into trouble.
- **D** He regrets some of the things he has done.

5 Why does John want to hear different music?
- **A** He doesn't share his aunt's taste in music.
- **B** He wants some music to reflect his mood.
- **C** He wants to cheer his uncle up.
- **D** He wants a change from the usual routine.

6 What impression do we get of Mimi in the text?
- **A** She is anxious and strict.
- **B** She is firm but caring.
- **C** She is kind but forgetful.
- **D** She is thoughtful and easy-going.

Saving our oceans

1 **You are going to read a magazine article about fourteen-year-old Dylan Vecchione, whose passion is to save coral reefs around the world. Read the article in <u>three minutes</u> and then tell a partner what information in the text you found surprising.**

Dylan is saving our oceans

Pollution is killing off coral reefs around the world. So Dylan, 14, is doing something about it – and he wants you to help.

Ever since Dylan Vecchione was a little boy, he has loved to swim, especially in the clear waters of Hawaii. Even though Dylan and his family live in Southern California, they take their holidays in Maui where Dylan likes to explore the underwater coral reefs.

(A) Dylan was seven when he first noticed that the once brightly-coloured coral was turning a sickly brown. It turned out that the brown colour came from algae, a result of pollution running off into the ocean. **1** ___ People stepped on the reef, ignorant of how delicate it was, and many people, including himself, covered themselves in sunscreen, unaware that there are toxins in the cream that can damage the reef. Dylan was devastated.

(B) Dylan realised he cared deeply about the reefs and wanted to know more about them. He found out that marine life, such as fish, lobsters, clams, sharks and sea turtles, relies on the reef to survive. **2** ___ Reefs are also important because they help protect the mainland from severe storms and flooding.

(C) The more Dylan discovered about what was harming Hawaii's reefs, the more he wanted to prevent it happening. He knew he had to do something to help. The following summer he asked to meet the manager at the hotel where he was staying and offered to write a brochure giving people advice on practical things they could do to look after the reef. **3** ___ To Dylan's astonishment, the manager said he would put a brochure in every room.

(D) Soon after, Dylan discovered that Hawaii's Division of Aquatic Resources, a government organisation dedicated to protecting the state's oceans, was already working to save the same reef. Dylan sent them an email, asking how he could help. An environmentalist, Darla White, wrote back and convinced Dylan of the importance of creating a virtual reef. If they could take enough photographs of the reef, they could track its health. Dylan never looked back. He set up his own organisation called ReefQuest. **4** ___ Dylan takes detailed underwater pictures of the Kahekili Reef off Maui and posts them online for scientists and students to study. His aim is to create a 'reef fingerprint' documenting reef conditions over time so scientists can make sure the reef isn't becoming uninhabitable for Hawaii's fish.

(E) Now when Dylan's family goes to Hawaii, he's not just on holiday. Dylan spends his time underwater taking photos for the Virtual Reef project or using a toothbrush to scrape the algae off. **5** ___ Organise a clean-up at your local beach or try to limit how much plastic you use as it can destroy underwater habitats. Although protecting the oceans is in everyone's best interests, Dylan knows that not everyone wants to have the same level of involvement as him. His work on the reef project has taught him that everyone can make a difference to their lives and the lives of those around them.

(F) So what is Dylan's advice? 'Identify your passion,' he says. 'Ask yourself what you love doing. If you want to change things, it needs to come from a real place. Find a mentor. I emailed lots of people who were already working to save the reefs to ask how I could help. They gave me so much great advice. Talk to adults – they actually listen to kids! **6** ___ I was surprised by how many adults, like the hotel manager, were excited to see a kid doing something to make the world a better place.'

2 **Work in pairs and answer the questions below. List the words that indicate what each paragraph is about. Underline these words in the article.**

a) Which paragraph talks about people who can help you?

Paragraph F. These words associated with people appear in this paragraph: mentor, adult, kid, hotel manager, people. There are also words to do with the topic of helping: help, gave great advice

b) Which paragraph in the article talks about the damage that is being caused to reefs?

....

....

c) Which paragraph talks about things you can do to help?

....

....

d) Which paragraph in the article talks about the usefulness of the reef?

....

....

e) Which paragraph talks about the goals of an online project that Dylan is involved in?

....

....

f) Which paragraph talks about the hotel where Dylan often stays?

....

....

EXAM TASK

3 **Six sentences have been removed from the article. Choose from the sentences A–G the one which fits each gap (1–6). There is one extra sentence which you do not need to use.**

A If you have an idea, don't be afraid to approach important people with it.

B Worse still, it was slowly killing the reefs.

C According to Dylan, everyone can do something small to help our oceans.

D There's nowhere he'd rather be.

E Some animals live on the reef which is a valuable source of food, while other animals find necessary shelter from predators in it.

F Its mission is to use the power of the internet to increase worldwide awareness about the state of the reefs.

G Dylan wanted to hand it out to guests on their arrival.

4 **Read through the text including the missing sentences to make sure it makes sense. How did looking at the topic words of each paragraph (in exercise 2) help you to do the exam task?**

Exam tip!

Look for topic connections between the words in the missing sentences and in the paragraphs. Underline these words as you do the task.

Mars by 2030!

1 Read the text below. What do you think it is about? Complete the first sentence with a, b or c.

a) Red Planet **b)** Great Red Spot **c)** Red Sea

Jupiter's .... is the most obvious feature on the planet. Scientists know that it is a truly giant storm, bigger even than Earth. Scientists are not so sure, though, why it is red. They think the red colour probably comes from phosphorus or sulphur in Jupiter's atmosphere.

On Earth, storms die out when they move over land. However, there is no solid landmass on Jupiter to cause this to happen. The storm also seems to be fuelled by heat from Jupiter, rather than the sun. All this means that there is no reason why the storm should die out. Surprisingly, scientists studying the Great Red Spot have noticed it is getting smaller. This may suggest that one day it will disappear completely.

2 Look at the underlined words in the text. Each of these words refers back to ideas in the previous sentence. What does each word or phrase refer to?

it (lines 2 and 3) .... All this (line 7) ....

They (line 3) .... This (line 9) ....

Fold here Fold here

3 Work in pairs. Fold the paper over so that you can't see the text in exercise 1. Look at these sentences from the text. Number them in the correct order.

- [ ] The storm also seems to be fuelled by heat from Jupiter, rather than the sun.
- [ ] However, there is no solid landmass on Jupiter to cause this to happen.
- [1] Jupiter's Great Red Spot is the most obvious feature on the planet.
- [ ] This may suggest that one day it will disappear completely.
- [ ] They think the red colour probably comes from phosphorus or sulphur in Jupiter's atmosphere.
- [ ] All this means that there is no reason why the storm should die out.
- [ ] Scientists are not so sure, though, why it is red.
- [ ] On Earth, storms die out when they move over land.
- [ ] Scientists know that it is a truly giant storm, bigger even than Earth.
- [ ] Surprisingly, scientists studying the Great Red Spot have noticed it is getting smaller.

4 Compare the two texts. Highlight the words in the sentences which helped you put them in order.

5 *However* and *also* are both used to link information in the text. Match each linker with three more which have similar meanings. Which are used 1) to give further information? 2) to signal a contrasting idea?

in addition nevertheless though too what's more yet

a) *however,* ....

b) *also,* ....

EXAM TASK

6 **Six sentences have been removed from the article. Choose from the sentences A–G the one which fits each gap (1–6). There is one extra sentence which you do not need to use.**

Mars 2030 or bust!

Meet sixteen-year-old Abby Harrison from Minneapolis in the USA. Abby is determined to be an astronaut one day. She tells us that you're never too young to start working towards your goals!

When Abby Harrison was little, her mum used to read a book to her about children who go to space. Abby was inspired by it and often stood in her garden, staring at the sky. 'I'd wonder "Where does the moon come from? How many stars are there?"' Abby tells me. 'I didn't understand the world around me, but I wanted to.'

In the seventh grade at her Minneapolis High School, Abby signed up for a course called 'Reach for the Stars'. **1** ___ The weekly course, which involved building model rockets and learning space history, culminated in a week-long space camp in Huntsville, Alabama. Following this experience, Abby's passion just continued to grow. She decided from that point on that she would do whatever it took to be an astronaut and it was then that she came up with her motto: Mars 2030 or bust! When Abby was asked to select a history project the following year, it was no surprise that she picked space history as her topic. She even bought a flight suit online to wear during the presentation.

At the end of that year, Abby asked her mum if it might be possible for them to watch one of the final launches of the space shuttle Endeavour. To Abby's amazement and delight, her mum agreed and a few days later they set off for Florida to visit the Kennedy Space Center. **2** ___ At the airport on the way home, Abby spotted a famous Italian astronaut, Luca Parmitano. Abby was unsure whether to introduce herself but finally plucked up the courage. She needn't have worried. Luca spoke to her for a whole hour, giving her essential advice about how to go about becoming an astronaut.

Luca and Abby stayed in touch via email. For Abby, it felt particularly special to have a real astronaut as a mentor. She'd tell him what she was learning at school and he'd tell her about his training for a May 2013 rocket launch in Kazakhstan. He was to be a flight engineer on a long-duration mission to the International Space Station. **3** ___ He had managed to get tickets to the rocket launch for Abby and her mum. 'I freaked out,' Abby tells me, laughing.

Abby's mother, who was a single mum, would have gone into debt to make sure her daughter could go to the launch. **4** ___ To pay for travel, Abby set up a fund-raising campaign on a site called RocketHub.com. First it was mostly family and friends who donated. Then Abby's followers on social media started to chip in. Even total strangers helped Abby out.

It was Abby's first time in another country and Kazakhstan was unreal. The launch itself was thrilling and she could feel the vibrations of the rocket engines in her chest and the heat on her face! Once Luca was in space, it was Abby who kept fans up-to-date with his progress via her own website, AstronautAbby.com. **5** ___ She also created a game called 'Catch Luca!' which encouraged followers to share photos they had taken of the International Space Station as it passed in orbit.

Abby has a bright future ahead of her. She is considering going to college to study engineering or biological science. But right now, her passion is to teach people as much as she can about space. She blogs as much as she can, and does video chats with classrooms across the country. **6** ___ Recently, when her younger sister Lily had a princess-themed birthday party, Abby showed up in her flight suit. And Lily loved it!

A She also loves showing other kids, especially girls, that it's OK to be interested in maths and science.

B Abby was one of about fifty students from local schools who took part in it.

C He was proud of Abby achieving her lifelong dream.

D Although Abby was blown away by everything there, for her the real thrill was to come later.

E Then one day, Abby got some news from Luca that she just could not believe.

F But in the end she didn't have to as Abby was determined to help fund the trip.

G By chatting with him on Twitter, she was able to report what he was doing in space.

Exam tip!

Highlight any referencing or linking words in sentences A–G. These will refer to information before and after the gaps in the text.

Three wishes and a dream job

1a Look quickly at the text below and answer the questions. The sentences are not in the correct order.

a) What kind of text do you think it is?

- magazine article
- a poem
- a story

b) Is the text

- serious?
- funny?

1b Discuss with a partner. What helped you reach your decision?

'Me first! Me first!' says the sales rep. 'I want to be in the Maldives, riding a jet ski without a care in the world.'

Whoosh! The office receptionist is gone.

'OK, now it's your turn!' the genie says to the manager.

The genie says, 'I have three wishes to give, so you can have one each.'

And the moral is: always let your boss speak first!

They rub the lamp to clean it and a genie comes out in a puff of smoke.

Whoosh! The sales rep is gone.

'Wow!' says the office receptionist. 'Me next! I want to be in Croatia, snorkelling in the clear blue sea.'

The manager says, 'I want those two back in the office after lunch.'

An office receptionist, a sales rep and their manager are walking to lunch when they find a rusty old oil lamp.

2 Fold the paper over so you can't see the correct answers. In pairs, decide on the correct order.

Fold here *Fold here*

3 Check your answers against the original story. Discuss with your partner what helped you put the sentences in the correct order.

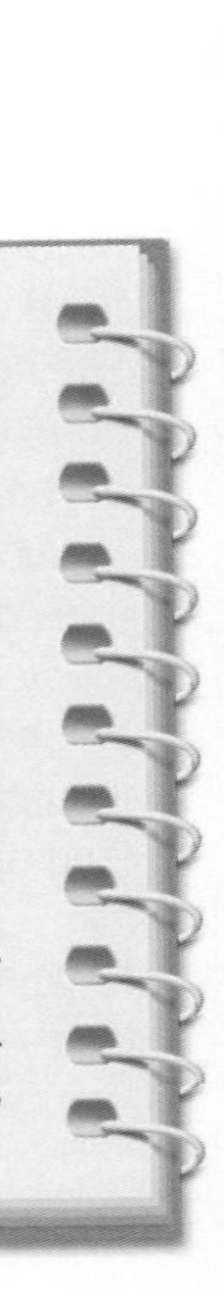

An office receptionist, a sales rep and their manager are walking to lunch when they find a rusty old oil lamp.

They rub the lamp to clean it and a genie comes out in a puff of smoke.

The genie says, 'I have three wishes to give, so you can have one each.'

'Me first! Me first!' says the sales rep. 'I want to be in the Maldives, riding a jetski without a care in the world.'

Whoosh! The sales rep is gone.

'Wow!' says the office receptionist. 'Me next! I want to be in Croatia, snorkelling in the clear blue sea.'

Whoosh! The office receptionist is gone.

'OK, now it's your turn!' the genie says to the manager.

The manager says, 'I want those two back in the office after lunch.'

And the moral is: always let your boss speak first!

4  **Read this text in two minutes. What is the aim of this article? Who is it written for?**

GETTING THE JOB YOU LOVE

Very often you only get one chance to show an employer you're the right person to employ. Why is the interview so important? 'The best candidate doesn't necessarily get the job: the best interviewee does,' says John Lees, author of *How to get a job you love*. Here are some tips to ace an interview.

1 Be mentally prepared. Ask yourself three questions: Why do I want this job? Why this organisation? What do I have to offer this company? In a recent survey, 63% of UK firms had concerns over finding enough skilled candidates. Find out what the company does, who their customers and competitors are, and what your responsibilities might be if you got the job. Zara, 22, learned the hard way that failure to prepare is preparation to fail. 'I'd been too busy to find out all I should have. I spoke to two people who knew the company and thought that was enough. I hadn't looked at their website before the interview, and it was full of new information. The person who interviewed me was incredulous I knew so little. He thought I was a waste of time.'

2 Many employers will ask you similar questions, so prepare your answers before you even walk into an interview. The classic ice-breaker is: 'Tell me about yourself.' It's your chance to share accomplishments, skills or hobbies that may be of interest to the employer. Be brief, specific and to the point. Employers may ask: 'Why do you want this job?' A good boss is hard to find. For example, 'I play several sports and have done a lot of research on sport products, so I have a good idea of what customers want from your sports shop.' 'What are your strengths and weaknesses?' State two or three of your strengths. Pick ones that match the job and choose a weakness that can be overcome, such as 'I'd like to have more skills / training in …'

3 Prepare questions to ask during the interview and be prepared to take notes. Ask questions that show you are conscientious and demonstrate you've researched – and are genuinely interested in – the company. Good ones include: 'I read about … can you tell me more about that?' 'Can you describe a typical day?' 'What training do you offer?' End with: 'When can I take my first holiday?'

4 Look professional. In a recent survey of UK companies, one top interview tip is dressing appropriately. Choose sports gear and trainers and avoid a suit. The right clothes will demonstrate that special care has been taken when attending the interview. 'Wearing too much jewellery or strong perfume or aftershave are a definite no,' advises Kath James, managing director of Luton Airport.

5 Greet the interviewer confidently with a smile, eye contact and a firm handshake. 'I favour people who show confidence and enthusiasm at an interview,' says Nazir Jessa, chairman of an electronics company. Nod and show your interest. Sit up straight and avoid off-putting body language like fidgeting or exaggerated hand gestures. Interviewers prize good communication skills and negatively rate the use of slang expressions or speaking without thinking. Speak clearly and avoid the temptation to talk too much. Make sure your answers are lengthy and detailed. Some interviewers use silence to see how you'll react. You can pass the lead back to them by pleasantly asking, 'Does that answer your question?' Don't interrupt the interviewer or say anything negative about previous jobs, colleagues or bosses.

6 A recent survey among UK employers produced their number one tip: Be yourself! Interviewees who try to exaggerate their abilities in order to impress an employer face trouble. 'I only speak English, but I always say I can speak French,' says graduate Ella Mitchel. Answer questions honestly, supporting what you say with specific examples of things you've done. If you don't understand a question, ask for an explanation.

5 **In each paragraph (1–6), there is a sentence that doesn't belong in this text. Can you find the six sentences? Why don't they fit?**

6 **Replace each of the wrong sentences with one of the sentences below. Choose from the sentences A–F the one which fits in each paragraph (1–6).**

A Keep your answers concise and relevant.

B End with: 'When can I expect to hear your decision?'

C Says property developer Adrian Gillooly, 'Those who try to cheat the process stand out.'

D Research the company on the Internet and through any personal contacts.

E Most employers agree that it's safer to overdress for an interview.

F Explain how your skills would help you do a good job.

Exam tip!

Always read through the text carefully once you have finished. Check that each paragraph makes sense.

Would you Adam and Eve it?

Cockney rhyming slang is a collection of phrases used by Londoners from the East End of the city. It started as a mid-nineteenth century code used by criminals to confuse the police, or by salesmen who didn't want their customers to understand what they were talking about. Rhyming slang involves replacing a common word (e.g. *look*) with a rhyming phrase of two or three words (e.g. *a butcher's hook*). But often the second word of the rhyming phrase is left out, (e.g. *a butcher's*).

1 Look at these examples of classic and modern cockney rhyming slang. Can you guess what the 'translations' are?

a) 'Can I have a Butcher's?' (from Butcher's hook) ......*Can I have a look?*......

b) 'Would you Adam and Eve it?' ....

c) 'Are you on your Jack?' (from Jack Jones) ....

d) 'Let's go for a Ruby!' (from Ruby Murray) ....

e) 'Like your Barnet!' (from Barnet Fair) ....

f) 'I'm going down the Fatboy.' (from Fatboy Slim) ....

g) 'He's still in his Barack Obamas.' ....

2 Work in pairs. These pairs of sentences are about the East End of London and Cockney rhyming slang. Look at each pair of sentences and decide which sentence should come first and explain why.

1 a) Cockneys were often working-class tradesmen who lived in London's East End. ☐

b) 'Cockney' came to refer to their accent and form of spoken English. ☐

---

2 a) A local politician says, 'It's really important we keep the older traditions alive and support them, not as fossils but as living traditions.' ☐

b) The dramatic growth of the East End has created a strong desire among East Londoners to preserve both the Cockney accent and rhyming slang. ☐

---

3 a) There are plans to teach it in the schools of East London. ☐

b) East Londoners have launched a campaign for Cockney rhyming slang to be recognised as an official dialect. ☐

---

4 a) Huguenots (who came from France in the sixteenth century), the Irish, Jews and more recently Bangladeshis and Somalis have all made their home here ☐

b) Since the 17th century, the East End of London has been a haven for immigrants. ☐

---

5 a) Immigrant groups brought with them the skills and traditions of their own cultures. ☐

b) This has created a vibrant world of street markets and shops with foods and goods from the world over. ☐

---

6 a) Shoreditch is now at the centre of the trendy London art and social scene. ☐

b) Shoreditch was once notorious for its run-down slums. ☐

---

7 a) One such square has been recreated as the setting for Eastenders, the BBC's longest-running TV soap opera. ☐

b) Some neighbourhoods are home to beautiful Victorian houses and tree-lined squares. ☐

3 In your pairs, choose the best sentence to follow a) and b). Choose from sentences 1 to 5.

a) The colourful and high-energy East End of London was once a string of quaint villages that sat to the east of the city's medieval wall. ....

....

b) Cockney is always changing and some slang has been updated so young people of today can understand it.

....

....

1 By the 19th century, it had become part of the fast-growing metropolis of London, a centre for docks, warehouses and factories.

2 There are many who say that the Cockney spirit of the East End is being lost as development moves ever forward.

3 The Bajan singer Rihanna has been driving her crew mad by learning Cockney rhyming slang.

4 'I'm going to the Fatboy' meaning 'I'm going to the gym' and 'He's still in his Barack Obamas' meaning 'in his pyjamas' are modern-day examples of rhyming slang.

5 Young professionals from all over Europe are buying run-down houses in the area and renovating them.

4 Now choose the best sentence to come before a) and b) below. Choose from sentences 1 to 5 in exercise 3.

a) ....

Some of these properties now appear in fashionable home and style magazines.

b) ....

'She's been reading phrases aloud in her best Cockney accent and finding it hilarious!' said a source close to the star.

Markets in the East End, then and now.

EXAM TASK

5 Read the article about London's East End. Six sentences have been removed from the article. Choose from the sentences A–G the one which fits each gap (1–6). There is one extra sentence which you do not need to use.

The changing world of London's East End

The East End of London was originally a collection of small villages and farmland outside the walls of the medieval City of London. It wasn't until the nineteenth century that the area became urbanised. When industrialisation came, it was rapid and the East End soon became a centre for docks, warehouses, factories and slums.

In 1828, the new St Katharine Docks opened to welcome shipments from Europe, the West Indies, Africa and the Far East. The Docks handled valuable cargoes, amongst them sugar, wine, tea, spices, perfume and marble. **1** ___ Buildings in the area were divided up to make small living spaces for these people. New buildings were constructed, but even so, the area was soon over-crowded and run-down.

In the nineteenth century, many of the residents of the East End lived in severe poverty. No laws protected their safety, employment or health. In 1866, a cholera epidemic took hold, killing 3,000 people. Unsurprisingly, crime and violence were commonplace. Robbers and criminals were notorious. **2** ___ In spite of this situation, or perhaps because of it, the local residents, known as 'Cockneys' became famous for their fighting spirit and humour.

The area also attracted immigrants, many of them refugees, and many of whom arrived at the local docks. Each group that arrived helped reshape the East End. **3** ___ The skills and diversity each group brought to the East End all contributed to this vibrant and exciting mix of cultures and languages that exists now.

Many of the docks were destroyed in the Second World War and this gave the area a chance for regeneration. The traditional industries of the East End died out as the area became modernised. Canary Wharf, with its iconic skyline, is home to Britain's banking and finance industry and was built on the site of one of the East End's busiest docks. **4** ___ In the 1980s and 1990s, the area re-invented itself as artists and designers moved into the low-rent warehouses. The area moved steadily upmarket and is now one of the trendiest parts of London.

British Indian writer Hari Kunzru grew up in the East End. He writes, 'Nowhere is the rapid mutation of the East End more visible than on Brick Lane.

When I first knew Brick Lane as a teenager in the 1980s, it was a tense place. **5** ___' Brick Lane is one of the most popular places to visit in the East End. It still has its bagel stalls, curry houses and sari shops. But the houses sell for millions of pounds and high fashion brands fight over shop space.

Not everyone supports the changes, least of all the locals. There are many who say that the Cockney spirit of the East End is being lost as development moves ever forward. The development of the industrial land around Stratford to build facilities and accommodation for the 2012 London Olympics helped transform the East End further. The Olympic building programme continues with plans to build several thousand more homes and create thousands of jobs by attracting businesses to the area. **6** ___ Many in the East End remain cynical about the benefits of the development for local residents.

A Yet, in spite of this, the East End still contains some of the worst poverty in Britain today.

B The East End docks were finally abandoned in 1980 and shipping moved down the Thames to Tilbury.

C The French Huguenots, for example, created a thriving textile industry.

D Large numbers of dock workers were needed for this.

E Now it is an established centre for youth-oriented consumer culture.

F Some of London's tallest and most exciting buildings are now here.

G None more so than Jack the Ripper, who carried out a series of awful murders in 1888.

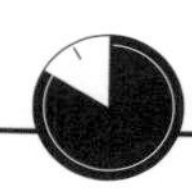

The truth about sugar

1 **Work in pairs. Look at the quiz questions and discuss.**

1 Do you get an energy boost from sugar?
Yes / No

2 Is sugar clearly indicated on food labels?
Yes / No

3 Is the sugar found in fruit (fructose) good for you?
Yes / No

4 Do sugar-free fizzy drinks help you lose weight?
Yes / No

5 Which is the best way to have less sugar in your diet?
Stop eating chocolate. / Stop having sweet drinks.

6 Is sugar addictive?
Yes / No

2 **Read the paragraphs and answer the questions (1–10). Underline the relevant words or phrases in paragraphs A–F.**

Which paragraph contains

1. a paraphrase for food labels?
2. another way of saying get an energy boost (a paraphrase)?
3. examples of alternative ways to describe sugar?
4. a synonym for sugar-free fizzy drinks?
5. examples of sweet drinks and chocolate bars?
6. two adjectives that suggest the opposite of an energy boost?
7. an adjective which is the opposite of good for you?
8. a synonym for have less sugar?
9. another way of saying addictive? (a paraphrase)
10. a phrase which is the opposite of lose weight?

A There are several different types of sugar, including glucose and fructose. Our bodies need glucose which is found in all natural foods. Fructose is found mainly in fruit and honey. But fructose is also added to processed food, and in these greater quantities can be harmful. Our bodies turn fructose into fat which is stored in the liver or released into our blood. Table sugar – the sugar that we add to our coffee – is half glucose and half fructose.

B You might feel a temporary lift after eating sweets (that's your blood sugar rising), but that's not the whole story. Sugar contains glucose which gives your body energy. The body then releases insulin which carries the glucose to the cells that need it and returns your blood sugar to normal. When that happens, your blood sugar may 'crash' and you'll feel sleepy. And when you are drowsy, you'll go looking for more sugar!

C Sugar is a feel-good substance. When we eat sugar, it releases dopamine – a chemical in our brains – which makes us feel happy. But if we eat sugar every day, the amount of dopamine released becomes less and so we need more sugary food to produce the same effect. In this way, sugar is almost like a drug.

(D) When you eat or drink something sweet, your brain expects sugar. If it doesn't get it – but gets artificial sweeteners instead – you may feel you need something with sugar as well. Believe it or not, there's actually a connection between drinking diet drinks and piling on the kilos.

(E) A large McDonalds Sweet Iced Tea contains more than thirteen teaspoons of sugar. A Grande Java Chip Frappuccino from Starbucks contains sixteen – that's more than double the amount in a Snickers or Dairy Milk bar! A lot of the sugar in our diets comes from what we drink. So that's a good place to start if you want to cut down on sugar.

(F) Don't expect 'sugar' to appear as the first ingredient on food product information. Food manufacturers are more clever than this. Some foods contain more than one kind of sugar and these will be listed separately. Malt syrup, sucrose, fruit juice concentrate – they're all names for added sugar which you can find on food labels. There are around forty different types of sugar or sugar substitutes used in processed food.

3 **Work in pairs. Match the questions in exercise 1 with the paragraphs in exercise 2. Which paragraph answers each question? Which words helped you match them?**

Exam tip!

In Part 7, look for synonyms (and their opposites), paraphrases and examples to help you complete the task. Circle the words in the article that help you match them to the questions.

EXAM TASK

4 **You are going to read about four people and their relationship with sugar. For questions 1–10, choose from the sections (A–D). The sections may be chosen more than once.**

Which person

explains the development of a habit? **1** ____

claims not to be concerned about their weight? **2** ____

intends to replace something in their diet with something else? **3** ____

argues that recommendations are unreasonable? **4** ____

compares their diet with someone else's? **5** ____

says their sugar total was more than they expected? **6** ____

is motivated by looking after others? **7** ____

mentions the companies that produce food? **8** ____

is recovering from an emotional upset? **9** ____

has been advised to make a change to their shopping habits? **10** ____

A I'm a father of two and I'm concerned about the amount of sugar in my kids' food. Cereal, pasta sauce and sweetened yogurts are all staples in our household and I've been told they should all go in the bin. I'm most concerned about breakfast. It's shocking how much sugar is hidden in an outwardly healthy packet of cereal. It's all very well for Hollywood stars to whip up an avocado and kiwi fruit smoothie, but how am I going to get that past my kids? I've even been told too much fruit is not good for you because it contains fructose. My kids eat lots of fruit: bananas, grapes and melon are all really sweet. But at least it's natural and contains fibre too. It's hard because your kids see their friends eating sugar all the time and I don't want them to feel left out.

B I didn't think I ate a large amount of sugar. I eat a healthy breakfast – scrambled egg on toast – no bowls of sweetened cereal or anything. I always have vegetables with my meal in the evening. A friend suggested I keep a food and drink diary. My diet was better than my friend's, but I discovered I'm still having around 28 teaspoons a day! I don't have enough energy to get through the day without having a boost from something sweet, but that's the same for everyone I know. I get real cravings for sweet drinks and can you believe half of the sugar comes from what I drink? Apple juice contains about six teaspoons of sugar, so I'm going to swap it for water. If I stop taking sugar in my tea too, then that's got to be a good thing.

C I took a healthy eating survey for fun, but I knew I was going to score quite high on sugar. I've got a really sweet tooth. I'm not worried that I'll get fat – my friends say I'm too skinny anyway – but I do want to be healthy. I'm only twenty and I reckon good habits now will set me up for the rest of my life. Unsurprisingly, my results showed I have 44 teaspoons a day. The World Health Organisation suggests around six teaspoons a day, but I think that's almost impossible. That's only one chocolate bar a day and no added sugar in the rest of your food. I'm not going to start checking food labels all the time or anything, but if I'm honest, I could probably go without the fizzy drink and the chocolate bar with my lunch. Leaving out those would cut 17 teaspoons of sugar from my day!

D Over the past five years my sugar intake has increased a lot. I started eating when I split up with my husband. It started with a treat to make myself feel better and before long I just had to have something sweet after every meal. I started to pile on the kilos and then my energy levels just fell away. Recently I decided to go on a detox programme. To start with I felt really drowsy and the cravings were awful, but now I feel better than I have done in months. I haven't cut out sugar altogether, but I am more aware of how much sugar I am consuming. I used to have two sugars in my morning cup of coffee, but now I just have one teaspoon on a Sunday. The worst thing about cutting down on sugar is the expense. Food without sugar is more expensive, but it's a small price to pay for your health. We need to support food manufacturers that do not add unnecessary sugars to their products.

Movie time trial

1 Work in pairs. Look at the films which are featured in the texts. Discuss the films with your partner. Have you seen any of these films? Did you like them?

A The Breakfast Club (1985)

This teen movie starred a group of unknown young actors, including Rob Lowe and Molly Ringwald, who later became famous as core members of Hollywood's Brat Pack. The film revolves around the amusing relationship between five teenagers – to quote the film's tagline: a brain, a beauty, a jock, a rebel and a recluse. The five meet for the first time in a Saturday detention class and discover they have more in common than they had imagined. This was the first teen 'group therapy' movie: by revealing each other's fears and differences, the characters realised they shared the common bond of adolescent confusion. *The Breakfast Club* was directed by John Hughes who was behind a number of teen flicks including *Pretty in Pink* and *Ferris Bueller's Day Off*. Although it did not win any awards, the film met with critical and commercial acclaim and has now achieved an almost cult-like status.

B Clueless (1995)

This 1995 movie starred Alicia Silverstone and Brittany Murphy, both of whom were relative unknowns. Silverstone's role of the spoiled airhead, Cher, steals the show. Cher is a high school student with bad grades and a heart of gold. She is clueless when it comes to current affairs, but she's talented at being popular. Cher and her rich friends rule a Beverly Hills high school. When a new student shows up, Cher sets out to prove herself by turning the girl into a fellow princess. Cher spends all her time matchmaking but soon realises she's the one who needs help. The plot is loosely based on the story of *Emma* by Jane Austen whose heroine is also wealthy and vain, but whose good heart also wins over the reader in the end. The movie turned the world of spoiled rich kids into a hilarious comedy. The film is an unusual combination of a satire with heart and captured the pulse of the money-crazed 90s.

C Mean Girls (2004)

Lindsay Lohan plays Cady Heron who has moved back to the USA after living in Africa for twelve years. Thrown into a high school environment for the first time, Cady finds herself having to choose between her new friends, the uncool Janis and Damian, and the Plastics, a hip and cool group of girls led by Regina. Cady finds an uneasy balance, but when Cady falls for Regina's ex-boyfriend, Aaron Samuels, things take a turn for the worse. The film was written by American comedian and actress Tina Fey and was inspired by her own high school experiences as well as Rosalind Wiseman's *Queen Bees and Wannabes*, a self-help book which explored school cliques. The script is full of often quoted one-liners such as 'On Wednesdays we wear pink.' Or 'I don't hate you 'cause your fat. You're fat 'cause I hate you!' *Mean Girls* explores the teen desire to do anything to be one of the cool kids, the need to seek out a group to which you belong and the effects of bullying.

D The Hunger Games (2011)

This movie is set in the fictional nation of Panem where every year a teenage boy and girl are sent from each of its twelve districts to compete in The Hunger Games. The Hunger Games are a nationally televised event in which participants must fight with one another until one survivor remains. Jennifer Lawrence stars as Katniss Everdeen, a great archer and hunter, who volunteers to take her younger sister's place in the contest. But Katniss is soon up against fighters who have been preparing for the Games for their whole lives. Jennifer Lawrence took on the role of brave and defiant Katniss in this film and its three sequels, and in the process became a reluctant role model. *The Hunger Games* films are based on the extremely successful novels by Suzanne Collins. The author also adapted her work for the screen and some critics have said that the film version would have benefited from being less faithful to the original book. The film contains some realistic and often shockingly nasty fight sequences but nevertheless this is a thrilling action movie.

2  **Play 'Time Trial'.**

- **Read the first question below. Underline the important words in the question. Now scan the texts and highlight the section where you think the answer is. You have thirty seconds.**
- **Now work with a partner to read the section more carefully and underline the word(s) that give you the answer. Write the answer in the box. You have thirty seconds to do this.**
- **Do the same for the other questions.**

Which review

1. talks about the teenage desire to fit in with others? ☐
2. considers that a film reflects an era? ☐
3. warns readers that they may find the film disturbing? ☐
4. is about a film that is partly based on a non-fiction book? ☐
5. has concerns about the use of the film's source material? ☐
6. suggests that the main character is someone we are unsure whether to like? ☐
7. centres on one film from a series? ☐
8. gives examples of the director's other work? ☐
9. discusses the box office success of the film? ☐
10. features a film character who wants to change the life of another? ☐

Super-fans

1 **How can you spot a super-fan? What sort of things do they do? Make a list of three things and share your ideas with the class.**

2 **Read the magazine article about celebrity culture. You have <u>three minutes</u>. Don't look up any unfamiliar words at this stage.**

3 **In your pairs, look at the words in bold in the text. Do you know any of them? Answer the questions in the call-out boxes.**

4 **Write definitions or guess the meaning of the following words.**

frantically	....	aspire	....
sulk	....	crushing	....
inaccessible	....	measure	....
all-consuming	....	blemish	....
alluring	....	obscurity	....

5 **Check your answers at the bottom of the page.**

Exam tip!

You may have to guess the meaning of unfamiliar words in the text. What part of speech is the new word? Do the surrounding words give you a clue to its meaning?

EXAM TASK

6 **Read the article about celebrity culture again. For questions 1–10, choose from the sections (A–D). The sections may be chosen more than once.**

Which paragraph mentions

a concern that teenagers are not setting their future goals high enough?	1	
a change that the writer finds strange?	2	
a suggestion that fame is not achieved easily?	3	
a relationship that is not equal?	4	
a reaction to not getting to do what you want?	5	
an unlikely outcome?	6	
an inconvenience caused by fan behaviour?	7	
celebrities who do not live up to expectations?	8	
a worry that teenagers are judging themselves too harshly?	9	
the sort of information fans find out about celebrities?	10	

KEY

1 *frantically* means hurriedly, in a way that shows you are very worried about a situation
2 *sulk* means to be angry but refuse to talk about what is upsetting you
3 *inaccessible* describes something or someone you can't reach
4 *all-consuming* describes something which you think about all the time
5 *alluring* means attractive
6 *aspire* means have a strong wish or hope for
7 *crushing* describes something that makes you lose hope or confidence
8 In this context, *measure* means judge
9 a *blemish* is a small mark on someone's skin
10 *obscurity* is not being known (an opposite of *fame*)

☆☆☆☆☆☆ Celebrity culture ☆☆☆☆☆☆

A It was a breezy, busy morning outside a store in New York City as tourists and shoppers edged their way around the loud mass of teens filling the street. Security guards worked to clear the pavements of girls who **frantically** checked their phones for updates. Their hair was perfect but they had bags under their eyes from sleeping on the pavement the night before. In just a few short hours, the security guards would cut the line in half. Those who got cut would put up a fight, cry or **sulk**. Those lucky enough to stay would have a chance of getting everything they had ever hoped for: thirty seconds with Kendall and Kylie Jenner.

'I'm pretty much their biggest fan ever,' said super-fan Michal, who still had six hours to wait until the Jenners' 5 pm arrival.

1 What part of speech is this word? What tells you this?

2 What part of speech is this word? What tells you this? Which words does it follow here? Are they the actions of happy people?

B There's been a shift in super-fandom in recent years. Celebs used to be glamorous but **inaccessible**, adored for their talents but completely out of touch with their fans. Now there's a weird familiarity. We call Katy and Niall by their first names, and, thanks to social media, we know what they ate for breakfast. In fact, stars sometimes feel like our best friends. But is this mostly one-way friendship just an innocent hobby? Or should we be more worried? Is it an **all-consuming** passion that is making us take our own dreams and ambitions less seriously? The idea of fame is so **alluring** that many young people would rather be near it than achieve their own success elsewhere. Jake Halpern, author of the book *Fame Junkies*, asked hundreds of teens what they most **aspire** to be. Do they have a strong wish to be a head of a major company, a Navy SEAL, a US senator, the president of a great university, or the personal assistant to a celebrity? Among girls, the most popular choice, by far, was the last one.

3 Is this a positive or negative adjective? Which two things tell you this?

4 What part of speech is this word? What tells you this? What verb is this word made from? What does the verb mean?

5 What other ideas in this sentence give you a clue to the meaning of this adjective?

6 There is a paraphrase to the meaning of this verb in the next sentence. What is it?

C Celebrities are often role models, especially for young people. In fact, celebrity obsession offers a way to express ourselves. Our choice of celebrity to follow sends a message to the world about who we are. So what happens when your beloved celebrity gets arrested or is accused of starting a fight? Stars are real people, after all, and if we are too wrapped up in their lives, it can be **crushing** when they fail. At the same time, the level of perfection they sometimes seem to achieve is not a fair standard to **measure** ourselves against. Remember they have a make-up team covering up every **blemish** and wear the latest expensive trainers so they always look cool.

7 What part of speech is this word? What tells you this? What verb does this word come from? Does this give you a clue to its meaning?

8 What part of speech is this word? What tells you this? Which words go with this word?

9 What part of speech is this word? What tells you this? Is this something people like to have? How do you know this?

D For some of us, following a celebrity is just the start. Even if your goal isn't to be a serious actor, you might dream about walking a red carpet one day. If so, you're not alone. One survey found that a quarter of teens say they don't just want – but expect – to be famous by the age of twenty-five. And it's not surprising, since many teens have skyrocketed from **obscurity** to fame as fast as you can say 'upload to YouTube'.

Jean Twenge, a psychologist at San Diego State University and the author of *Generation Me*, points out that sudden fame looks as if it has been reached with minimal effort, but 'statistically, it's very rare to become famous and most of those people work very hard to get there'.

10 This noun is contrasted with another noun in this sentence. What is it?

Fantasy tales

Student A

1 **Read the text about Philip Pullman's trilogy of books, *His Dark Materials*. In your notebook, write questions to find out the missing information.**

Example: *What is the name of the poem by John Milton?*

Philip Pullman is the author of *His Dark Materials*, a trilogy of books. The books are a reworking of the famous poem **(1)** .... written by John Milton in the seventeenth century. The **(2)** .... book in the trilogy is *Northern Lights*.

Northern Lights tells the story of a young orphan girl called Lyra who lives at **(3)** .... in Oxford with her dæmon. Dæmons are the physical manifestation of a person's 'inner-self' and take the form of **(4)** .... Lyra's life is turned upside down when children, including her best friend, Roger, start to go missing. Lyra sets off to the North with the Gyptians – **(5)** .... – on a voyage of discovery where she discovers **(6)** .... and why the children are disappearing.

Philip Pullman's books have an amazing ability to make you think fantasy is real. Once you've started reading Philip Pullman's trilogy, you won't **(7)** ....

Northern Lights was made into a film called *The Golden Compass*, starring Nicole Kidman and **(8)** ....

In the 'Big Read', a survey of the UK's favourite books conducted by the BBC, Pullman's trilogy came third.

2 **Now ask Student B your questions on *His Dark Materials* and complete the information in the text.**

3 **Student B will ask you some questions about this text on J.R.R. Tolkien's trilogy of books, *The Lord of the Rings*. Scan the text to find the information.**

Exam tip!

In Part 7, read the questions before you read the text. Scan the text to find the answers to the questions.

The Lord of the Rings is a trilogy of books written by J.R.R. Tolkien during the 1950s. The trilogy is set in the fictional land of Middle Earth. It follows the journey of Frodo Baggins. Frodo Baggins is a hobbit. Hobbits are fictional characters, similar to humans but much smaller. Frodo is on a mission to save Middle Earth from the evil Sauron and, in order to do this, Frodo must destroy the One Ring by throwing it into the volcano Mount Doom.

J.R.R. Tolkien

The Lord of the Rings is an epic story of Good versus Evil, and in Middle Earth Tolkien creates an amazing alternative world which even has its own language and history.

The Lord of the Rings trilogy was made into a series of films directed by Peter Jackson in his native New Zealand and starring Elijah Wood as Frodo Baggins. The series is said to have had a budget of around 300 million US dollars. Unsurprisingly, the special effects were exceptional and the series as a whole was very successful. The final film in the series, *The Return of the King*, won eleven Academy Awards.

Student B

1 Read the text about J.R.R. Tolkien's trilogy of books, *The Lord of the Rings*. Write questions to find out the missing information.

Example: *When was the trilogy written?*

The Lord of the Rings is a trilogy of books written by J.R.R. Tolkien during the **(1)** .... The trilogy is set in the fictional land of Middle Earth. It follows the journey of Frodo Baggins. Frodo Baggins is a hobbit. Hobbits are **(2)** .... Frodo is on a mission to **(3)** .... from the evil Sauron and, in order to do this, Frodo must destroy the One Ring by **(4)** ....

The Lord of the Rings is an epic story of Good versus Evil, and in Middle Earth Tolkien creates an amazing alternative world which even has **(5)** ....

The Lord of the Rings trilogy was made into a series of films directed by Peter Jackson in his native **(6)** .... and starring Elijah Wood as Frodo Baggins. The series is said to have had a budget of around **(7)** .... US dollars. Unsurprisingly, the special effects were exceptional and the series as a whole was very successful. The final film in the series, **(8)** .... , won eleven Academy Awards.

2 Student A will ask you some questions about this text on Philip Pullman's trilogy, *His Dark Materials*. Scan the text to find the information.

Exam tip!

In Part 7, read the questions before you read the text. Scan the text to find the answers to the questions.

Philip Pullman is the author of *His Dark Materials*, a trilogy of books. The books are a reworking of the famous poem *Paradise Lost* written by John Milton in the seventeenth century. The first book in the trilogy is *Northern Lights*.

Philip Pullman

Northern Lights tells the story of a young orphan girl called Lyra who lives at Jordan College in Oxford with her dæmon. Dæmons are the physical manifestation of a person's 'inner-self' and take the form of an animal. Lyra's life is turned upside down when children, including her best friend, Roger, start to go missing. Lyra sets off to the North with the Gyptians – riverboat travellers – on a voyage of discovery where she discovers who her parents are and why the children are disappearing.

Philip Pullman's books have an amazing ability to make you think fantasy is real. Once you've started reading Philip Pullman's trilogy, you won't be able to stop.

Northern Lights was made into a film called *The Golden Compass*, starring Nicole Kidman and Daniel Craig. In the 'Big Read', a survey of the UK's favourite books conducted by the BBC, Pullman's trilogy came third.

3 Now ask Student A your questions on *The Lord of the Rings* and complete the information in the text.

EXAM TASK

4 **You are going to read an article in which four students talk about their favourite science-fiction book. For questions 1–10, choose from sections (A–D). The students may be chosen more than once.**

Which student mentions that the book they read

is set in an actual city?	1
could be considered old-fashioned?	2
is suitable for fans of the work of another author?	3
initially put them off?	4
is the best in a series?	5
was recommended by someone else?	6
has some characters who are both animal and human?	7
has memorable place names?	8
raises issues about the characters' actions?	9
involves a fight between humans and beings from outer space?	10

A *MORTAL ENGINES* Philip Reeve

I have read all Philip Reeve's books in the Predator Cities series and *Mortal Engines* is my favourite. It follows the fortunes of city boy Tom Natsworthy. Tom looks up to the archaeologist Thaddeus Valentine and longs to go on similar adventures, but when a disfigured outcast girl, Hester, tries to kill Valentine, Tom's world is really turned on its head. The story is set in a world where giant cities become predators and our civilisation is barely remembered. This is a thrilling adventure story, but the characters are strong and believable and we never lose sight of their story and the moral dilemmas they find themselves in. Readers who have enjoyed Philip Pullman's fiction will also love this.

B *THE WAR OF THE WORLDS* H.G. Wells

H. G. Wells' classic science-fiction adventure is set in South London and tells the story of an invasion from Mars. The story is narrated by an unnamed protagonist who sees the Martian war machines rain down from space. The Martians are highly developed wormlike creatures which suck blood. The reader follows the narrator's narrow escapes while he tries to figure out what has happened. H. G. Wells wrote this book at the end of the nineteenth century and it is one of the earliest stories that talks about a conflict between mankind and aliens from another planet. Some of the language is hard for a modern reader to follow and the science is largely out-of-date but it is still a very good read.

C *PERDIDO STREET STATION* China Miéville

This book is very different from any other I've read and it's hard to know whether to classify it as science fiction or fantasy. Unlike Miéville's first novel, *King Rat*, which was set in London, this story takes place in the fantasy metropolis of New Crobuzon. I found New Crobuzon horrifying and brutal but I never tired of reading about its bizarre inhabitants, like the *khepri*, a race of women with insect bodies for heads and the *cactacae* or cactus-people. The names of the suburbs and streets, including Perdido Street station itself, build a vivid sense of place you want to stay in and find out more about. This is just as well because the book is over 800 pages long!

D *DUNE* Frank Herbert

I don't read much science fiction and when I first read this, I couldn't get past the first few pages. There were so many made-up characters and terms. But a friend who loved the book persuaded me to try it again and this time I was blown away. *Dune* is set on a fictional desert planet called Arrakis where huge sand-worms live and produce a mind-altering substance called 'melange'. The story is a battle between the Atreides family and their enemies for control of the planet and the 'melange'.
If you love escaping to a fantasy world, then this book is for you. Frank Herbert wrote this book in 1965 and there are five further books in the series. His son, Brian, co-authored still more books based on notes found after his father's death.

CAMBRIDGE ENGLISH
Language Assessment
Part of the University of Cambridge

Do not write in this box

Candidate Name
If not already printed, write name in CAPITALS and complete the Candidate No. grid (in pencil).

Candidate Signature

Examination Title

Centre

Supervisor:
If the candidate is ABSENT or has WITHDRAWN shade here

Centre No.

Candidate No.

Examination Details

0	0	0	0
1	1	1	1
2	2	2	2
3	3	3	3
4	4	4	4
5	5	5	5
6	6	6	6
7	7	7	7
8	8	8	8
9	9	9	9

Candidate Answer Sheet

Instructions

Use a PENCIL (B or HB).

Rub out any answer you wish to change using an eraser.

Parts 1, 5, 6 and 7:
Mark ONE letter for each question.

For example, if you think **B** is the right answer to the question, mark your answer sheet like this:

0 A B C D

Parts 2, 3 and 4:
Write your answer clearly in CAPITAL LETTERS.

For Parts 2 and 3 write one letter in each box. For example:

0 EXAMPLE

Part 1

1	A	B	C	D
2	A	B	C	D
3	A	B	C	D
4	A	B	C	D
5	A	B	C	D
6	A	B	C	D
7	A	B	C	D
8	A	B	C	D

Part 2

		Do not write below here
9		9 1 0 u
10		10 1 0 u
11		11 1 0 u
12		12 1 0 u
13		13 1 0 u
14		14 1 0 u
15		15 1 0 u
16		16 1 0 u

Continues over →

FCE R

DP802

Part 3

		Do not write below here
17		17 1 0 u
18		18 1 0 u
19		19 1 0 u
20		20 1 0 u
21		21 1 0 u
22		22 1 0 u
23		23 1 0 u
24		24 1 0 u

Part 4

		Do not write below here
25		25 2 1 0 u
26		26 2 1 0 u
27		27 2 1 0 u
28		28 2 1 0 u
29		29 2 1 0 u
30		30 2 1 0 u

Part 5

31	A	B	C	D
32	A	B	C	D
33	A	B	C	D
34	A	B	C	D
35	A	B	C	D
36	A	B	C	D

Part 6

37	A	B	C	D	E	F	G
38	A	B	C	D	E	F	G
39	A	B	C	D	E	F	G
40	A	B	C	D	E	F	G
41	A	B	C	D	E	F	G
42	A	B	C	D	E	F	G

Part 7

43	A	B	C	D	E	F
44	A	B	C	D	E	F
45	A	B	C	D	E	F
46	A	B	C	D	E	F
47	A	B	C	D	E	F
48	A	B	C	D	E	F
49	A	B	C	D	E	F
50	A	B	C	D	E	F
51	A	B	C	D	E	F
52	A	B	C	D	E	F

denote 0121 520 5100

READING AND USE OF ENGLISH PRACTICE PAPER

Part 1

For questions **1–8**, read the text below and decide which answer (**A, B, C** or **D**) best fits each gap. There is an example at the beginning (**0**).

Example:

0 **A** looking **B** facing **C** meeting **D** dealing

0	A	B	C	D
	☐	■	☐	☐

Cat Island

We hear a lot these days about the problems that wild life is **(0)** .... More and more animals are on the verge of extinction because of changes to their **(1)** .... , hunting and other dangers. **(2)** .... , there are places in the world where animals are thriving in the wild and Cat Island in Japan is just one of them. Recently tourists have been flocking to visit this small, remote island in southern Japan which is completely dominated **(3)** .... cats. They outnumber the population of **(4)** .... human residents by six to one. **(5)** .... the cats were first brought to the island to do what they do best – kill the mice on the fishermen's boats. Then they stayed and **(6)** .... Now, the cats live in small colonies all over the island in old, abandoned buildings and are regularly fed by the fishermen and people on the island. They have no **(7)** .... predators on the island and so they roam fearlessly everywhere. The Japanese people have a special affection for cats and believe that they **(8)** .... luck. The cats on Cat Island are definitely very lucky animals indeed!

	A	B	C	D
1	**A** houses	**B** regions	**C** habitats	**D** surroundings
2	**A** Although	**B** However	**C** Despite	**D** Therefore
3	**A** from	**B** of	**C** at	**D** by
4	**A** antique	**B** mature	**C** elderly	**D** ancient
5	**A** Apparently	**B** Recently	**C** Fortunately	**D** Especially
6	**A** extended	**B** multiplied	**C** developed	**D** repeated
7	**A** common	**B** natural	**C** usual	**D** biological
8	**A** fetch	**B** deliver	**C** spread	**D** bring

Part 2

For questions **9–16**, read the text below and think of the words which best fits each gap. Use only **one** word in each gap. There is an example at the beginning (**0**).

Write your answers **IN CAPITAL LETTERS**.

Example: | 0 | I | S |

What – no music?

For many actors and singers, part of the pressure of performing **(0)** .... remembering words. Audiences don't see them glancing at notes or pieces of paper **(9)** .... prompts written on them. However, it's a different story for another type of performer – the musician. With a **(10)** .... rare exceptions, musicians read music from music stands. This is, in itself, a difficult skill, but once mastered it relieves the pressure of relying **(11)** .... memory when on stage. The Aurora Orchestra, however, have done something **(12)** .... few musicians, especially large groups, have done before. They have twice performed **(13)** .... symphony completely from memory. Last year it was a Mozart symphony and this year a Beethoven. **(14)** .... to their conductor Nicholas Collon, performing music from memory is **(15)** .... extremely difficult and rewarding. It allows the musician **(16)** .... freedom in interpreting the music and communicating with the audience. It sounds an amazingly brave thing to do, but a very dangerous one! A tiny memory lapse from one member of the orchestra could affect the playing of every person in the group.

Part 3

For questions **17–24**, read the text below. Use the word given in capitals at the end of some of the lines to form a word that fits in the gap **in the same line**. There is an example at the beginning (**0**).

Write your answers **IN CAPITAL LETTERS**.

Example: | 0 | F | I | T | N | E | S | S |

Give it a go!

Everyone knows that doing sports is important for our health and **(0)**	*FIT*
However, many people need some **(17)** .... This is where 'Give it a go!', a	*ENCOURAGE*
(18) ....event on Hampstead Heath, can help. The event gives people the	*YEAR*
opportunity to try out new sports for free. This year visitors to the event had the chance	
to try out an **(19)** .... form of tennis. Three-a-side tennis is enormous fun!	*INNOVATION*
You have to be quick on your feet and quick thinking too as it's so **(20)**	*PREDICT*
In traditional tennis the players play to their natural **(21)** .... , but in three-a-side	*STRONG*
the players need to work as a team of three and this creates a **(22)** .... new type	*COMPLETE*
of game. Tennis has always been a popular sport but it has its **(23)** .... It can be	*ADVANTAGE*
very expensive to join tennis clubs and there is limited **(24)** .... of public tennis	*AVAILABLE*
courts. With three-a-side, all you need is a copy of the rules, some line marking equipment	
and a special T3 net. Then a group of friends can play anywhere.	

Part 4

For questions **25–30**, complete the second sentence so that it has a similar meaning to the first sentence, using the word given. **Do not change the word given**. You must use between **two** and **five** words, including the word given. Here is an example (**0**).

Example:

0 My favourite aunt gave me this laptop.

GIVEN

I .... my favourite aunt.

The gap can be filled by the words 'was given this laptop by', so you write:

Example: | **0** | *WAS GIVEN THIS LAPTOP BY* |

Write only the missing words **IN CAPITAL LETTERS**.

---

25 The match has probably started so it's not worth going now.

POINT

The match has probably started so .... now.

26 The teacher didn't let us leave the classroom until we had finished the exercises.

MADE

The teacher .... before we left the classroom.

27 My sister regrets not working harder for her exams.

WISHES

My sister .... harder for her exams.

28 I last saw Danny three days ago.

FOR

I .... three days.

29 The boss will only promote you if you work hard.

UNLESS

The boss will .... work hard.

30 I told Maria that I was sorry I had lost her book.

APOLOGISED

I .... her book.

Part 5

You are going to read an extract from a story in which a young woman called Carrie talks about looking for a new flat. For questions **31–36**, choose the answer (**A, B, C** or **D**) which you think fits best according to the text.

It's strange how radically a person's tastes can change over the years. I'd always imagined myself settling down with my (improbably handsome and rich) future partner in an idyllic cottage in an unspoilt and isolated part of the countryside – preferably with an extensive garden and stunning views over rolling hills to the distant sea. Perhaps that's a dream that most of us covet and that lurks at the back of our minds until we actually face the reality of finding somewhere practical to live. Then other priorities take over, and we're forced to accept that the limitations of money and access to work and other important amenities figure much more strongly as we investigate the properties available.

I had certainly never expected to be seriously considering buying an ultra-modern flat, in an ultra-modern tower block in the centre of a soulless modern town to live in for the foreseeable future. But there I was with my partner Connor (shortish, plumpish and quite poor), and our smart estate agent, outside the front door to Flat 3, Floor D of Marley Court.

'You'll love it!' he gushed. His gushing was getting on my nerves a little. This was the fourth property we'd seen so far that morning and at each property he had expressed his opinion that we would be mad to let it 'slip away', because the market was 'on fire' at the moment and we would never have such a 'unique opportunity' again. I tuned him out and concentrated on assessing the cleanliness of the corridor and smartness of the front door. I met Connor's eyes and he winked at me. I felt laughter bubbling up inside me but firmly pushed it down. This was definitely not a good time to get the giggles.

The agent pushed his key into the lock and the door swung open. The hall was impressive with high ceilings and a smart, clean, elegant look and it lead into a spacious open plan space with a living and kitchen area. I was slightly surprised by the total absence of pictures or homely touches anywhere in the flat but this was explained away by the agent who informed us that the owner had moved out a month previously, although *line 22* that didn't explain why the furniture was still in place. I guess the owner maybe wanted to try to sell it to whoever bought the flat.

Before I could voice my queries the agent had taken Connor out onto the balcony that overlooked the rear gardens of the building with a view across to the river. As I looked round the stark whiteness of the room I started to have misgivings about buying somewhere with such little character and the seeds of my old dream began to blossom once again. I pushed the thoughts away and started to mentally tick off boxes – good cupboard space, nice tiles, upmarket fittings, lovely stone-coloured worktop with …? I looked again. There was a trace of something red on the stone worktop. Had someone been eating a jam sandwich?

I joined the others on the balcony. Our agent was in the middle of enthusing over the view.

'An opportunity to get a property with a view like this is very rare! And just think, you can move in whenever you're ready. There's no chain. The owner has already bought another place and moved out. It's been empty for quite a long time so I'm sure you could get a good deal.'

I felt a faint chill on my shoulders. You probably know the feeling – as if someone's staring at you from behind and you have to turn round. I turned round, but all I could see was the next balcony along and it was completely empty. Then my eyes were drawn down to my hand on our balcony rail. I was touching something sticky. There was another trace of red all along the top of the rail. This time I was sure that it wasn't jam.

31 Carrie believes that our attitude towards the type of house we want to live in changes because

A our dream homes don't actually exist.

B our expectations change as we get older.

C our decisions are affected by external requirements.

D our relationships require compromises.

32 How does Carrie feel about the flat she is going to view?

A She's disappointed that it is a modern flat.

B She's surprised that she is looking at modern flats.

C She is depressed that she has to buy something modern.

D She is confused by the range of flats she has viewed.

33 Why does the estate agent irritate Carrie?

A He uses language that she doesn't understand.

B He is trying to force them to buy something they don't want.

C He repeats the same things over and over again.

D He isn't always very truthful.

34 In 'although that didn't explain' in line 22, 'that' refers to the fact that

A there aren't any indications of anyone living in the flat.

B the flat is still fully furnished.

C the owner vacated the flat several weeks ago.

D the previous occupant preferred an uncluttered living area.

35 What starts to concern Carrie as she looks round the flat?

A It might not be what she really wants.

B It will not live up to her expectations.

C It reminds her of somewhere she used to live.

D It doesn't meet her requirements.

36 On the balcony Carrie becomes aware

A that they are alone in the flat.

B that a previous speculation was wrong.

C that someone is watching her from another flat.

D that they are in a dangerous position.

Part 6

You are going to read a magazine article about the problem of homelessness for young people in the UK. Six sentences have been removed from the article. Choose from the sentences **A–G** the one which fits each gap (**37–42**). There is one extra sentence which you do not need to use.

Homelessness: a serious problem

Imagine being cold, hungry and having nowhere to sleep. The sad truth is that this is the reality for thousands of people in Britain today. Homelessness is not a new problem – there have always been people who have fallen on hard times and ended up with no home – but it is incredible to think that it is still happening today. It is even sadder to realise that it is not just older adults who end up in this situation but thousands of teenagers too.

When we think of people being 'homeless', we automatically think of those sleeping in the streets. **37** ____ For example, they might be in a temporary hostel or bed and breakfast accommodation, or staying with lots of different people or in unsafe or unsuitable accommodation, like an illegal squat (an empty property that has been taken over by homeless people). Being homeless can be described as a situation where you have 'no fixed abode' – no permanent place to live.

A young person may become homeless for a variety of reasons. **38** ____ But there are other reasons young people become homeless. These include money problems, for example not being able to pay rent, problems related to gangs and friends or exclusion from school.

One young person, Adam, found himself sleeping on the streets after moving from Leeds to London. **39** ____ 'All I thought was that I have nothing and I'm worth nothing,' says Adam. It was winter and a harsh time to be sleeping rough but Adam continued for eight months, sleeping under bridges until a charity found him a place to stay.

In Britain the problem is rising. **40** ____ Research has shown that the cost of each homeless person to the country is in excess of £26,000. There is a cost to the health service and the criminal justice system, expensive temporary accommodation, and long periods on welfare. This means that it is in everyone's interest to solve the problem of homelessness.

One organisation that is dedicated to helping young homeless people aged between sixteen and twenty-five is the charity Centrepoint, which was set up in 1969. The organisation not only provides help and support with accommodation but with many other things too. Health is a big issue for homeless people. **41** ____ In addition to this, homeless people need to be able to move forward. This means providing educational opportunities – such as the chance to study or learn a new skill which will enable them to find jobs in order to support themselves.

Charities like Centrepoint need financial help to keep going. **42** ____ Others argue that being homeless is a person's own fault and not something we should need to respond too. They are wrong. Statistics show that millions of people are just a few steps away from losing everything – loss of employment can lead to non-payment of rent which can lead to loss of accommodation which can lead to break up of family which can lead to .... yes, sleeping on the streets.

A Unfortunately many of us find it uncomfortable to think about a problem which can, quite literally, be on our doorsteps.

B Homelessness affects around 80,000 young Brits every year and as well as affecting each individual, it also has an indirect effect on the rest of the population.

C Although many young homeless people have experienced this, they might also be homeless in other ways.

D It may be down to mental problems that the person has become homeless in the first place, and living on the streets also takes its toll physically.

E Many charities run sponsored sleep-outs where people are sponsored by friends and family to sleep out on the streets for one night to raise money.

F After a row with his partner he walked out and being too proud to ask his friends for help, he slept out on the streets.

G Family breakdown is often a major factor – six out of ten young homeless people report that they had to leave home because of arguments, violence, relationship breakdown or being told to leave.

Part 7

You are going to read an article about short breaks. For questions **43–52**, choose from the sections (**A–C**). The sections may be chosen more than once.

In which section does the writer mention

the particular skills required by people who go on a break?	**43**
the benefits for everyone involved in a break?	**44**
the origin of a type of break?	**45**
encouraging people to communicate and integrate?	**46**
restrictions on the opportunities to go on a break?	**47**
specific rules about what can be taken on a break?	**48**
a link between a feature of the locality and a name?	**49**
providing necessary distraction for people?	**50**
reaching a destination by public transport?	**51**
offering participants an alternative to another free-time activity?	**52**

Breaks with a difference

A If you're feeling stressed, a short break from routine and work is often the answer. Most people would head for the beach or a shopping spree in a big city but many office workers in Tapei, the capital of Taiwan, have found another way to chill out, and one which appears at first to be rather contradictory! A couple of hours on the bullet train east of Taiwan brings you to a small village which is home to some members of the Jinpu tribe. City workers come here, not to relax but to work. Because of a lack of employment opportunities most of the young people from the village have moved to bigger towns and cities, leaving older residents who are not always able to do the jobs necessary to keep their village looking smart and in good condition. Tourists can come to the village for a four-day working holiday and in exchange for food and accommodation, they do important DIY chores around the village such as repainting the buildings in the traditional bright orange paint that gives another meaning to the nickname the Jinju people have been given: 'Sons of the Sun'! The residents are quick to point out that in order to keep a good balance between tourism and normal village life, the numbers of people coming on these working breaks are limited and the events only happen twice every summer.

B The popularity of computer gaming has played an important part in the recent increase in city-break escape games. For the uninitiated, this is where people use clues and solve puzzles to escape from locked rooms. Yes, people really do pay to be locked in a room! The craze started in 2006 in the US and was inspired by the works of Agatha Christie, the famous detective novelist. Now it is possible to find these attractions in cities all round the world – in Budapest alone more than 30 room-escape games have opened recently. The people who are attracted by the games are often students or young professionals who need a break from their busy and stressful lives. Apparently the games, which require participants to be observant and use their critical-thinking skills, offer a welcome relief from work-related stress by imposing a completely different kind of pressure! They also provide a real life context to the sort of games that people usually play on computers, allowing the players the physical interaction with a puzzle that online games cannot give. So, if you fancy finding your way out of a prison cell, a locked museum room or an Egyptian tomb, your fantasy is waiting for you! And you probably won't have to travel far to indulge.

C A short break in the countryside might be just what a lot of us need after weeks of working or studying hard. However, the idea behind the short breaks offered by 'Unplugged Weekends' is not to chill out on walks through fields and forests or relax in a hotel pool with sessions and treatments in a spa. 'Unplugged' refers specifically to the unplugging of digital devices! These weekend breaks are designed for those who have become addicted to digital technology and any access to phones or computers is forbidden. Throughout their stay the participants are bombarded with alternative activities to take their minds off the fact that they are no longer physically attached to their devices. There are exercise classes, cultural activities and (surprise! surprise!) old fashioned face-to-face conversations. In addition to this, the weekend helps counter the modern addiction to technology by giving tips on how to establish a better balance in our lives. Is your phone ringing as you read this? Or maybe you've just had a notification from your social media website? Go online immediately – to sign up for one of these breaks!

Answers

Part 1

Play fifty-fifty (pages 6–7)

1 **a)** The correct answer is *laid*.
laid is the past simple form of *lay* meaning to put down; *lay* is the past simple form of *lie* meaning to put your body flat; *lied* is the past simple form of *lie* meaning to not tell the truth and *let* means allow or allowed.

b) The correct answer is *beat*.
You *win* a match, *beat* a team and *score* a goal or point; to *beat a team by two points* means there is two points difference between the two teams; *lose* is the opposite of *win*

c) The correct answer is *recognised*.
remember and *recall* both mean to call back from memory, but in this sentence *recognise* is the correct verb as this means to know who someone is or what something is because you have seen it or them before; we *remind* someone *to do something, e.g. I reminded Marcus to go to the bank.*

d) The correct answer is *presently*.
presently means 'in a short time'; *at the moment* means 'now'; *at present* and *nowadays* both mean 'these days' – *nowadays* is in contrast to how things used to be in the past, e.g. *This area used to be very safe, but there are a lot of burglaries here nowadays.*

e) The correct answer is *amount*.
amount and *number* refer to how much there is of something: *amount* is used with uncountable nouns, a *number* can be counted; *size* refers to how big something is and *rate* refers to the number of examples of something or the speed at which something happens, e.g. *the rate of unemployment, the rate of change. Rate* could be used in this sentence if it was rephrased as follows: *Environmentalists are very concerned about the rate at which pollution is being dumped in the sea.*

f) The correct answer is *Despite*.
Although and *However* would be used with a different sentence structure: *Although the running team didn't have a track to practise on, they finished first. The running team didn't have a track to practise on. However, finished first. Despite* is followed by a noun or in this case a gerund acting as a noun (*having*). *Whereas* is used to compare and contrast, e.g. *Whereas the team from Hamilton had no track to practise on, the team from Holloway have a brand new stadium.*

2 **a)** The correct answer is *Both*.
Both is used to talk about two people or things. *All* is use to talk about a number of people or things. *Neither* and *every* are used with a singular noun: *neither* (parent) means 'not one or the other' and *every* (parent) is used t refer to all the parents in a particular group. *Neither* can be used with a plural noun if it is followed by *of*, e.g. *Neither of my parents.*

b) The correct answer is *brought*.
In this context, *bring* means 'take the ticket to where yo are now'; *take* would mean 'go to another place with the ticket'; *fetch a ticket* would mean 'go to another place ar come back with the ticket', so you do not need *with you* with *fetch*; *obtain* means get something that you want and is usually quite formal, e.g. *He obtained permission from the bank.*

c) The correct answer is *contrary*.
on the contrary is used to give more information about a negative statement you have made; *on the other hand* and *in contrast* are used to contrast two statements; *qui the opposite* is an alternative to *on the contrary.*

d) The correct answer is *earn*.
earn a living means to work and get enough money to live; *earn* is used to talk about money you get from work *gain* can be used to talk about getting something you want, e.g. *gain a qualification; receive* means to get, often when talking about a gift, letter or message; *collec* has a number of meanings including to go to a place to take someone or something away, e.g. *They collected their passports from the office.*

e) The correct answer is *succeeded*.
We use *succeed* with *in* + gerund to mean do something you tried or wanted to do; *manage to do something* means to succeed in doing something difficult; we can use *achieve* with a noun – it is used for something good or important, e.g. *achieve an aim; win* means to be the best or most successful in a match or competition, etc.

f) The correct answer is *noticed*.
You *watch* something; you *notice* something is there when you see, hear or feel it; *observe* suggests that you have been studying it carefully; *remark* is to give your opinion on something you have seen.

The common cold (page 8)

4 **1** B **2** A **3** B **4** D **5** A **6** D **7** C **8** B

Telling barefaced lies (page 9)

1 **a)** 6 **b)** 2 **c)** 7 **d)** *not used* **e)** 4 **f)** 5 **g)** 3 **h)** *not used* **i)** 1

2 **A**

keep your head down means avoid being noticed or getting involved in something, e.g. *I'm just getting on with my work and keeping my head down.*
catch someone red-handed at something means catch someone in the act of doing something wrong, e.g. *The police caught the robbers red-handed.*
be up to your ears in something means to have a lot of something, e.g. *I'm up to my ears in work.*

B

stick your neck out means to give your opinion on something without worrying about what others think, e.g. *I'm sure this is the right thing to do, so I'm happy to stick my neck out.*
be up in arms about something means be very angry about something and prepared to fight for it, e.g. *Everyone is up in arms about the plans to build new houses here.*
get cold feet means to not feel brave about something, e.g. *She's getting married next month but she's starting to get cold feet.*

C

keep an eye on someone or something means to watch something carefully especially if you are concerned about something, e.g. *The coach is keeping an eye on her results this year.*
pull someone's leg means to tell someone something that isn't true for a joke, e.g. *I don't believe it. You're pulling my leg!*
have the cheek to do something means to be rude or not show respect, e.g. *The waiter service was terrible and then they had the cheek to ask me for a tip!*

D

turn a blind eye to something means to pretend not to see something, e.g. *I knew my young cousin was upset, so I turned a blind eye to his behaviour.*
break someone's heart means to upset someone badly, e.g. *It broke my heart when they cut the old tree down.*
have no stomach for means to not want to do something, e.g. *The soldiers had no stomach for a fight.*

On my way (pages 10–11)

a) direction: *direction* here means the general way in which you move **b)** way: in this context, *way* means a distance or length of time **c)** paths: *path* can be used to talk about a way through life; if *your paths cross*, you meet someone by chance (idiom) **d)** way: *way* here means a road or path, etc. that you take to get somewhere
e) track: tracks (n) are the marks left on the ground from an animal, person or vehicle; *to be on the track of* is to be searching for or hunting for someone or something
f) path: when a lot of people walk over the same piece of ground a *path* or *track* is formed; a *path* can also be made on purpose, e.g. *a concrete path.* **g)** way: *the way back* is a common collocation to mean going back to the place where you started **h)** directions: *directions* are instructions about how to get to a place **i)** track: *on the right track* is an expression which means *doing or thinking the right/wrong things* **j)** way: *work your way up* is an idiom which means to achieve something by working

5 **1** D **2** D **3** A **4** A **5** B **6** D **7** C **8** C

Part 2

Your smartphone – best friend or worst enemy? (pages 12–13)

2 **1** d **2** f **3** e **4** a **5** g **6** b **7** c

3 **a)** someone **b)** a **c)** who **d)** do **e)** worse than **f)** from **g** so

4 Some suggested answers:
Text A:
pronoun: ***everywhere*** *you look, Try* ***it****!*
article: ***the*** *world around us, watch* ***a*** *movie, on* ***a*** *school trip*
relative pronoun: ***which*** *means,*
substitution: *live without* ***one****;* comparative phrase: *just* ***as*** *powerful as*
preposition: *world* ***around*** *us, depend* ***on*** *my phone, use …* ***for***
emphasis: *I can't* ***even*** *watch,* ***just*** *as powerful*

Text B:
pronoun: *encourage* ***us*** *to think, we hear* ***others****,* ***nobody*** *at my school does*
article: ***the*** *best,* ***an*** *infinite source,* ***a*** *great way*
relative pronoun: *people* ***who*** *have the same interests*
substitution: *nobody at my school* ***does****;*
comparative phrase: *the same interests* ***as***
preposition: *talking* ***about****, know nothing* ***about****, take part* ***in*** *the conversation, connect* ***with***
emphasis: ***really*** *love,* ***even*** *take part*

Having fun for free (pages 14–15)

3 **1** about **2** at **3** to **4** for **5** with **6** in **7** like **8** from

Pick a card! (pages 16–18)

2 **1** get **2** to **3** up **4** around/out **5** are **6** out **7** going **8** with

So you want to be a fashion designer ... (page 19)

1 **a)** I've always **been** quite artistic ...
b) No, it was**n't** my ambition when I was at school.
c) My tutor because he told me not **to** get interested in fashion!
d) When he told me it would be too difficult, I **was** absolutely determined to do it!
e) If you want go into fashion because you love clothes and shopping, you probably **will** not do that well.
f) To succeed you **must** be desperate to create something.
g) I think about fashion **all** the time – I never stop.
h) Be prepared to work for free or on very low pay for a number **of** years.
i) Success **never** happens by chance ...
j) ... and that includes **going** to a really good fashion school.

2 **a)** *was*
b) *been*
c) *you **will** probably not, you **must** be desperate*
d) *told me not **to**, includes **going***
e) *not, never*
f) *all (the time), a number of*

3 **1** held **2** moving / coming / going **3** no / not **4** been **5** to **6** can **7** does **8** all

Part 3

Walking on air (pages 20–21)

1 They are all used in extreme sports.

2 **A** BMX racing started in the early 1970s in southern California. This form of off-road racing on bikes is now one of the most **well-known** extreme sports. There are many **international** events for the, often **teen/teenage**, participants and unsurprisingly, it is fiercely **competitive**. For those who say the sport is not extreme enough, there is the challenge of performing stunts. Judging by the injuries at the end of each competition, this sport is definitely extreme, always **exciting** and definitely **dangerous**.

B The extreme sport of highlining is becoming increasingly **popular**, thanks to the **dramatic** images available online. To do this sport you need to be **brave**, but also very **athletic** since you will be balancing on a nylon line less than an inch **wide** which is suspended high above the ground. Highlining requires both **physical** and mental strength. Breathing and movements need to be **controlled**. 'Each and every move you make must be perfect. It's like walking on air,' says twenty-six-year-old Jon Fait.

C Running away from an **angry** bull is not everyone's idea of a fun activity, but for some **thrill-seeking** individuals, this sport is not to be missed. The bull-running festivals take place in a number of towns in Spain, Portugal and Mexico. The bull run in the Spanish city of Pamplona is world-famous. The bulls are led through the streets to the bull ring by runners. They run for 825 metres which usually takes about three or four **terrifying** minutes. For those who don't want to be in the streets, **amazing** views of this very dangerous spectacle can be had from high up on the balconies of the houses in the old quarter.

3 **1** sensational **2** snowy **3** skilled / skilful **4** enthusiastic **5** expensive **6** wonderful **7** adventurous **8** sociable

4 -able, e.g. available, sociable
-ible, e.g. incredible
-ic, dramatic, athletic, enthusiastic
-ing, e.g. exciting, thrill-seeking, terrifying, amazing, tempting
-ful, e.g. wonderful, skilful
-ous, e.g. dangerous, (world-) famous, adventurous
-y, -ly, e.g. angry, snowy, necessary, early
-ive, e.g. competitive, expensive
-ed, e.g. controlled, disappointed, tried, tested, skilled, faint-hearted
-al, e.g. international, physical, mental, sensational

5 well-known (past participle), teen/teenage, extreme, popular, brave, wide, high, perfect, fun, great, alone, online

Two cities (pages 22–23)

1 **a)** impossible **b)** overcrowded **c)** discontented **d)** underrated **e)** unlikely **f)** unaffordable

2 Other prefixes in the text that mean the same as *un-* are *dis-* and *im-* (these prefixes all mean 'not'). Another prefix that has the same meaning is *-in*. Before adjectives beginning with 'm' we use *im-* instead of *in-*. The same applies for adjectives beginning with 'l' (*il-*) and 'r' (*ir-*).

4 **1** unforgettable **2** unfair **3** illegal **4** unemployed **5** over-priced **6** unaffordable **7** underpaid (also low-paid or lower-paid) **8** overcrowded

Making friends (page 24)

2 brilliance, cheerfulness, confidence, disorganisation, encouragement, hardness / hardship, honesty, imagination, impatience, intelligence, kindness, loneliness, loyalty, optimism, patience, popularity, selfishness, wisdom

3 -ance / -ence -dom -ism -ity / -ty / -y -ment -ness -ship -sion / -tion
The following nouns all appear in exercise 1: *quality, personality, ability, maturity, disappointment, happiness, advice, relationship, occasion*. Other examples for *-ism* are *pessimism, racism, symbolism*. Other examples for *-dom* are: *boredom, freedom, kingdom*.

4 **1** skills **2** confidence **3** kindness **4** encouragement **5** belongings **6** preference **7** activities **8** disagreements

5 *preference, activities, disagreements, skills* and *belongings* don't fit into any of the groups.

Word dice (page 25)

1

Verb:	Noun form:	Adjective form:
act	action / activity	active
advise	advice	advisable
anger	anger	angry
behave	behaviour	well-behaved / badly-behaved
brighten	brightness	bright
choose	choice	chosen
clean	cleanliness	clean
concern	concern	concerned
contrast	contrast	contrasting
control	control	controlling / controllable
darken	dark / darkness	dark
deepen	depth	deep
demand	demand	demanding
die	death	dead / deadly
doubt	doubt	doubtful / dubious
empty	emptiness	empty
frighten	fright	frightened
give	gift	giving
heighten	height	high
help	help	helpful / helpless
introduce	introduction	introductory
know	knowledge	knowing / knowledgeable
legalise	law	legal
lengthen	length	long
like	like	likeable
live	life	alive / lively / live / living
lose	loss	lost
marry	marriage	married
practise*	practice	practical / practising
predict	prediction	predictable
produce	product	productive
prove	proof	proven
save	safety	safe
see	sight	seen
shorten	shortage / shortness	short
speak	speech	spoken
strengthen	strength	strong
succeed	success	successful
think	thought	thoughtful / thoughtless
vary	variation / variety	various / varied
weaken	weakness	weak
widen	width	wide

*This verb is spelt 'practise' in UK English, but 'practice' in the USA.

2 **1** natural **2** various **3** predictions **4** legal **5** success **6** activities **7** introduction **8** shorten

Part 4

Your turn! (pages 26–27)

Student A

1 **1** c **2** e **3** f **4** a **5** b **6** d

2 **a)** He reminded me to turn off the headlights.
b) My sister apologised for not ringing before.
c) I haven't filled in the form yet.
d) It's bound to rain if we have the party outdoors!
e) I can't afford a holiday this year.
f) They had no difficulty (in) finding a buyer for their flat.

Student B

1 **1** e **2** f **3** c **4** a **5** b **6** d

2 **a)** My cousin advised me to pack an extra jumper.
b) I regretted not speaking to him earlier.
c) I didn't expect it to be such a heavy bag.

d) The manager must have been very angry when he found out.
e) The building work took more time than I had hoped.
f) I've never been so frightened (in my life).

Earthquakes in Nepal (pages 28–29)

1 **1** About a quarter of the population has been affected by two earthquakes in Nepal.
2 On April 25 2015, Nepal was hit by a massive 7.8 magnitude earthquake.
3 Entire villages have been destroyed.
4 Just seventeen days later the disaster was followed by a second quake.
5 A large number of ancient monuments in the capital, Kathmandu, were damaged.
6 Hundreds of thousands of people were made homeless by the quake.
7 A fifteen-year-old boy was rescued from the debris of a seven-storey building.
8 A medical worker said it was miraculous. The boy had been under the rubble for 120 hours.
9 A very old man was found under the rubble. He is thought to be 101.
10 A journalist at the scene reported that he had only suffered minor injuries.
11 A tourist who was just north of the capital said the earthquake had been pretty scary. Snow and rocks and houses had started coming down.
12 A spokesperson from the Nepal Tourism Board told us that they hoped the return of tourists would restore the lives of people there.
(Note that items 10 and 11 could be left in past simple)

3 **1** is said to be
2 are thought to have gathered
3 was also seriously damaged
4 had to be rebuilt
5 told me he felt / feels lucky
6 the quake being scarier

Notice this! (page 30)

2 **1 a)** Patients without an appointment **can't be seen** by a doctor.
b) Patients with no appointment **are not able to see** a doctor.
2 a) Dogs **must not** use the beach.
b) Dogs **are not / aren't allowed (to go)** on the beach.
3 a) Applications **have to / need to be** received by 10th July.
b) It **is necessary to submit / send your application** by 10th July.
4 a) The council **does not / doesn't / will not / won't let you** park here.
b) You **are not / aren't / are never permitted to park** here.
5 a) A valid form of ID **is required when you collect / to collect** your order.
b) You **have to show a** valid form of ID when you collec your order.
6 a) Customers **can leave** a 10% tip if they want to.
b) Customers **don't have to leave** a 10% tip.
7 a) You **should take out insurance** before the trip.
b) You **ought not to travel** without insurance.
8 a) Students who arrive after 8.45 **will need to / have t sign** the late book.
b) It **is essential that students** who arrive after 8.45 sig the late book.

Hedgehogs and bats (page 31)

1 **a)** catch sight of **b)** on the look-out **c)** going down **d)** take care of **e)** die out **f)** make up **g)** cope with **h)** broken up **i)** run over **j)** take part in

2 **1** look down on **2** to run out of **3** put up with **4** up my mind to build **5** bats make use of the

Part 5

Reading between the lines (pages 32–34)

1 **1** d **2** a **3** f **4** c **5** b **6** e

2 **b)** Ten: Una and Geoffrey Alconbury, Mary Poppins, Julie Enderby, Mavis Enderby, Jamie, Daddy, Malcolm and Elaine Darcy and their son, Mark.

3 **a)** Bridget is not looking forward to the party. We know this because she says it is the 'last thing on Earth' she fee she can do. She says her mother 'forced [her] to promise to go.'
b) Bridget says she is 'exhausted' by the conversation an is 'puzzling' over it. She 'bellows' at her mother. She uses the phrases 'desperately' and 'panicked wildly'.

5 **a)** 2 The correct answer is D.
b) 5 The correct answer is B.
c) 1 The correct answer is C.
d) 4 The correct answer is A.
e) 3 The correct answer is B

Kevin's secret (pages 35–37)

4 **1** B **2** C **3** D **4** D **5** B **6** A

5 C

6 **1** C; For Part 5 of the exam, it is a good idea to read the relevant sections of the text again before trying to answer the questions. The differences between the options can be subtle so students should get into the habit of reading these parts of the text very carefully.
2 B; One way of approaching the task is to read the question, not look at the options and predict what the answer is. Students can then see if their prediction matches any of the multiple-choice options and think about why the other answers are not correct. Students need to keep an open mind about the answer, though, and be prepared to change their ideas if necessary.
3 C; The answers can be quite tricky and it is a good idea for students to be able to explain why the other answers are not correct.

A new Golden Age? (pages 38–39)

a) W **b)** A **c)** W **d)** A **e)** E **f)** A **g)** W **h)** E **i)** E **j)** A **k)** E **l)** W

1 B **2** A **3** C **4** B **5** A **6** D

Article: *to have misgivings, a bit embarrassed, got on each others' nerves*
Multiple-choice questions: *uneasy, irritated, awkward*

Nowhere Boy (pages 40–41)

Mimi was John Lennon's aunt. John Lennon was brought up by his aunt Mimi and her husband George. George died when John was fourteen.

a) glanced **b)** repeated **c)** if it bothered him **d)** tough **e)** a distraction **f)** lucky **g)** get in the way of **h)** oblivious

1 D **2** A **3** C **4** C **5** B **6** B

Part 6

Saving our oceans (pages 42–43)

b) Paragraph A. These words about damage appear in this paragraph: *sickly, algae, pollution, harm, toxins, damage.*
c) Paragraph E. These words which indicate things you can do appear in this paragraph: *organise, try to limit.* There are also words about helping: *level of involvement, make a difference.*
d) Paragraph B. These words about advantages of the reef appear in this paragraph: *marine life, sharks and sea turtles rely on, important, protect.*
e) Paragraph D. These words describing an online project appear in this paragraph: *organisation, ReefQuest, posts them online.* There is also the word *aim* which is a synonym of *goal.*
f) Paragraph C. These words about the hotel appear in this paragraph: *manager, hotel, staying, room.*

3 **1** B **2** E **3** G **4** F **5** C **6** A

Mars by 2030! (pages 44–45)

1 Great Red Spot

2 *it* refers back to Jupiter's Great Red Spot / storm; *They* refers back to the scientists; *All this* refers back to the reasons which have been given explaining why the storm should not die out; *This* refers back to the evidence that the Great Red Spot is getting smaller.

4 The referencing pronouns and articles (*it, they, this, the*) help with ordering the sentences. Use of linking words (*also, though, However*) and adverbs (*Surprisingly*) also help to connect the text.

5 **a)** however, nevertheless, though, yet
b) also, in addition, too, what's more
Group a is used to signal a contrasting idea.
Group b is used to give further information.

6 **1** B: *it* refers back to the 'Reach for the Stars' programme.
2 D: *later* refers forward to the meeting with Luca.
3 E: *some news* refers forward to Luca getting the tickets.
4 F: *she* refers to Abby's mother.
5 G: This sentence gives an example of how Abby kept fans up-to-date. The sentence which follows this uses *also* to introduce another example.
6 A: *also* introduces an additional goal that she has.

Three wishes and a dream job (pages 46–47)

1 **a)** This is a story. Even though the text is not in order the length of the text and the characters are clues. Even on a quick-read, you may have noticed story vocabulary, such as *moral, genie, lamp* and use of an opening narrative tense *are walking … when.*
The story is funny: the number of exclamation marks and the cartoon illustration indicate this.

2/3 **b)** The conventions of story-telling and of the Aladdin story will help with this task: the characters are listed at the beginning of the story; the moral of the story comes at the end; the lamp is rubbed before the genie appears; the genie speaks to offer wishes and the characters reply a wish at a time. Some of the clues in the story itself are the words 'first' and 'next'.

4 The article gives tips on giving a good interview for a dream job. It is aimed at someone who is preparing for an interview, possibly someone who is going to their first interview.

5 Paragraph 1: In a recent survey 63% of UK firms had concerns over finding enough skilled candidates. (This is a sentence from a different article about UK employers.)
Paragraph 2: A good boss is hard to find. (This sentence talks about the employer rather than the interviewee.)
Paragraph 3: End with: 'When can I take my first holiday?' (This sentence would not be appropriate advice.)
Paragraph 4: 'Choose sports gear and trainers and avoid a suit.' (This sentence contradicts later information in this paragraph.)
Paragraph 5: Make sure your answers are lengthy and detailed. (This contradicts what was previously said in this paragraph.)
Paragraph 6: 'I only speak English, but I always say I can speak French,' says graduate Ella Mitchel. (This contradicts what was previously said in this paragraph.)

6 Paragraph 1: D Paragraph 2: F Paragraph 3: B
Paragraph 4: E Paragraph 5: A Paragraph 6: C

Would you Adam and Eve it? (pages 48–50)

1 **a)** 'Can I have a **Butcher's**?' (from **Butcher's hook**) means 'Can I have a **look**?'
b) 'Would you **Adam and Eve** it?' means 'Would you **believe** it?'
c) 'Are you **on your Jack**?' (from **Jack Jones**) means 'Are you **on your own / alone**?'
d) 'Let's go for a **Ruby**!' (from **Ruby Murray**) means 'Let's go for a **curry**!' Ruby Murray was an Irish singer who had hits in the UK in the 1950s.
e) 'Like your **Barnet**!' (from **Barnet Fair**) means 'Like your **hair**!' Barnet Fair is an annual fair that has taken place in North London since the sixteenth century.
f) 'I'm going down the **Fatboy**.' (from **Fatboy Slim**) means 'I'm going down the **gym**.' This modern example of rhyming slang refers to an English DJ famous in the 1990s.
g) 'He's still in his **Barack Obamas**.' This modern example of rhyming slang means 'He's still in his **pyjamas'**.

2 **1** a, b
The second sentence explains more about a term that was introduced in the first sentence. 'their' in the second sentence refers back to 'Cockneys' in the first sentence.
2 b. a
The quotation comes second as it supports the first sentence.
3 b, a
'it' in the second sentence refers back to Cockney rhyming slang in the first sentence.
4 b, a
The general statement in the first sentence is followed by specific examples in the second.
5 a, b
The second sentence explains the effect of the first. 'This' in the second sentence refers back to the situation in the first.
6 b, a
It is common for texts to follow a chronological order, in this case the first sentence refers to the past and the second to now.
7 b, a
The first sentence is general, leading to a particular example in the second. The phrase 'One such square' introduces the particular example.

3 **a)** 1: The history of the area is being described in chronological order.
b) 4: The second sentence uses examples to back up the general statement in the first sentence.

4 **a)** 5: We move from the general to the specific in these two sentences.
b) 3: The first sentence is followed by an amusing quote the second.

5 **1** D (The sentence following this tells us more about the dock workers.)
2 G (The general statement about notorious criminals is followed up with an example.)
3 C (The information about immigrant groups leads to the particular example of the French Huguenots.)
4 F (Sentence F gives a further example of how the area has been modernised.)
5 E (The first part of the quote is about Brick Lane in the past and the second part refers to now.)
6 A (Sentence A keeps to the topic of wealth, poverty and benefits, but puts the opposite view, which is introduced by *yet*.)

Part 7

The truth about sugar (pages 51–53)

2 **1** F *food product information* **2** B *feel a temporary lift* **3** F *malt syrup, sucrose, fruit juice concentrate* **4** D *diet drinks* **5** E *McDonalds Sweet Iced Tea, Grande Java Chip Frappuccino, Snickers, Dairy Milk* **6** B *sleepy, drowsy* **7** A *harmful* **8** E *cut down on sugar* **9** C *like a drug* **10** D *piling on the kilos*

3 1 B 2 F 3 A 4 D 5 E 6 C
The words that helped students to match the questions and paragraphs are the examples, paraphrases and synonyms that students underlined in exercise 2. They will also use same content words to help in matching, such as 'fructose' in question 3 and paragraph A.

4 1 D 2 C 3 B 4 C 5 B 6 B 7 A 8 D 9 D 10 A

Movie time trial (pages 54–55)

2 1 C 2 B 3 D 4 C 5 D 6 B 7 D 8 A 9 A 10 B

Super fans (pages 56–57)

3 **1** *frantically* is an adverb
2 *sulk* is a verb; in this context it follows *put up a fight* and *cry* – these are the actions of frustrated or disappointed people
3 *inaccessible* is a negative word. We know this because it follows *but* which indicates that it is not a positive word like glamorous; the use of the prefix *in-* is most often used with negative words.
4 *all-consuming* is an adjective; it comes from the verb *consume* which means to eat or use up
5 *alluring* describes the way fame attracts young people. We know this because it has an *-ing* ending and is describing fame.
6 *aspire* means the same as *have a strong wish to*. This paraphrase appears in the next sentence.
7 *crushing* is an adjective; we know this because it has an *-ing* ending and is describing the noun *passion*; it comes from the verb *crush*, meaning to 'press something so hard that it breaks' e.g. *you can crush a can in your hand; crushing* means 'very disappointing and hard to deal with'
8 *measure* is a verb; it is used with *a standard* and is followed by *ourselves* and *against* here, i.e. measure ourselves against a standard
9 *blemish* is a noun, it is preceded by *every*; we know that this is not something people like to have from the context: they cover up every blemish
10 *obscurity* is contrasted with *fame* in this sentence

1 B 2 B 3 D 4 B 5 A 6 D 7 A 8 C 9 C 10 B

Fantasy tales (pages 58–60)

Student A, suggested questions:
1 What famous poem did John Milton write?
2 Which book in the trilogy is *Northern Lights*?
3 Where does Lyra live in Oxford?
4 What does a daemon take the form of?
5 Who are the Gyptians?
6 What does Lyra discover?
7 What will happen once you've started reading the trilogy?
8 Who starred in *The Golden Compass* with Nicole Kidman?

Student B, suggested questions:
1 When did J.R.R. Tolkien write the trilogy?
2 What are hobbits?
3 What is Frodo's mission?
4 How must Frodo destroy the One Ring?
5 What does Tolkien's alternative world have?
6 Where did Peter Jackson film the series?
7 How much did the film series cost to make?
8 What was the title of the final film in the series?

4 1 B 2 B 3 A 4 D 5 A 6 D 7 C 8 C 9 A 10 B

Reading and Use of English Practice Paper

Part 1

1 C 2 B 3 D 4 C 5 A 6 B 7 B 8 D

Part 2

9 with **10** few **11** on **12** which / that **13** a **14** According **15** both **16** more

Part 3

17 encouragement **18** yearly **19** innovative **20** unpredictable **21** strengths **22** completely **23** disadvantages **24** availability

Part 4

25 there is / there's no point going **26** made us finish the exercises **27** wishes (that) she had worked **28** have not / haven't seen Danny for **29** not promote you unless you **30** apologised to Maria for losing

Part 5

31 C 32 B 33 C 34 C 35 A 36 B

Part 6

37 C 38 G 39 F 40 B 41 D 42 A

Part 7

43 B 44 A 45 B 46 C 47 A 48 C 49 A 50 C 51 A 52 B

Material written by: Fiona Davis

Practice test written by: Lynda Edwards

Publisher: Jacquie Bloese

Development Editor: Sarah Silver

Editor: Judith Greet

FCE Consultant: Lynda Edwards

Designer: Sylvia Tate

Cover Design: Eddie Rego

Picture Research: Amparo Escobedo

Picture credits:
The common cold: delihayat/iStockphoto
Telling barefaced lies: MaszaS/iStockphoto
On my way: elisalocci/iStockphoto
Your smartphone – best friend or worst enemy?: S. Chiang, McEntire, I. Çiydem/iStockphoto
Having fun for free!: sanjagrujic/iStockphoto
So you want to be a fashion designer ... : DM. Benett, T. Fewings/Getty Images
Walking on air: P. Walter, D. Ramos/Getty Images; S. Bachlakov/Shutterstock; A. Conway/iStockphoto
Two cities: compassandcamera, AndreyGatash/iStockphoto
Earthquakes in Nepal: O. Havana/Getty Images
Notice this!: no_limit_pictures, T. Messick/iStockphoto
Hedgehogs and bats: GlobalP/iStockphoto; R. Jay/Shutterstock
Reading between the lines: Universal/Everett/REX
Kevin's secret: Tim Soter
A new Golden Age?: M. Tama/Getty Images
Nowhere boy: CBS Photo Archive/Getty Images
Saving our oceans: crisod / iStockphoto
Mars by 2030!: 3quarks/iStockphoto; M. Stewart/WireImage/Getty Images
Three wishes and a dream job: Dave Smith/Beehive illustration
Would you Adam and Eve it?: S. Sexton/Hulton Archive/Getty Images; J. Greig/iStockphoto, E. Dijour/Shutterstock
The truth about sugar: OHoffmann, Julichka, kiboka, Popartic, C. Whitman, baona, DRB Images, LLC, 3bugsmom/iStockphoto
Movie time trial: Buyenlarge/Getty Images; Paramount, Lions Gate/Everett Collection/REX; MarsBars/iStockphoto
Super-fans: J. Merritt/Getty Images
Fantasy tales: H. Magee, MJ Kim/Getty Images; alvarez, ValuaVitaly, xijian, XiXinXing/iStockphoto

The publishers are grateful to the following for the permission to reproduce copyright material: Page 33: Extract from *Bridget Jones's Diary*, Helen Fielding (Macmillan); Pages 40-41: Extract from *Nowhere Boy* (Scholastic UK) © Lennon Films Ltd, Channel Four Television and UK Film Council.

Printed in the UK by Bell & Bain Ltd, Glasgow